Nick Vando...

iPad
for Seniors

in
easy steps

10th edition
covers all versions of iPad with iPadOS 14
(including iPad mini and iPad Pro)

In easy steps is an imprint of In Easy Steps Limited
16 Hamilton Terrace · Holly Walk · Leamington Spa
Warwickshire · United Kingdom · CV32 4LY
www.ineasysteps.com

Tenth Edition

In Easy Steps Limited supports The Forest Stewardship Council (FSC),
the leading international forest certification organization. All our titles
that are printed on Greenpeace approved FSC certified paper carry the
FSC logo.

MIX
Paper from
responsible sources
FSC
www.fsc.org   FSC® C020837

Printed and bound in the United Kingdom

ISBN 978-1-84078-909-6

Contents

1 Choosing your iPad

It's compact, it's stylish, it's powerful; and it's perfect for anyone, of any age. This chapter introduces the iPad, its different models, the iPadOS 14 operating system and its interface, and some of the basic controls and functions, so you can quickly get up and running with this exciting tablet.

The iEverything

The iPad is a tablet computer that has gone a long way to change how we think of computers and how we interact with them. Instead of a large, static object it is effortlessly mobile, and even makes a laptop seem bulky by comparison.

But even with its compact size, the iPad still manages to pack a lot of power and functionality into its diminutive body. In this case small is most definitely beautiful, and the range of what you can do with the iPad is considerable:

- Communicate via email, video and text messaging.

- Surf the web wirelessly.

- Add an endless number of new "apps" from the Apple App Store.

- Use a range of entertainment tools, covering music, photos, video, books and games.

- Do all of your favorite productivity tasks such as word processing, creating spreadsheets or producing presentations.

- Organize your life with apps for calendars, address books, notes, reminders, and much more.

Don't forget

"Apps" is just a fancy name for what are more traditionally called programs in the world of computing. The iPad has several apps that come built in and ready for use. There are thousands more available to download from the online App Store (see Chapter 5, pages 96-100).

The New icon pictured above indicates a new or enhanced feature introduced with iPads using iPadOS 14.

Add to this up to 10 hours' battery life when you are on the move, a range of different sizes (with a Retina Display screen of outstanding clarity) and a seamless backup system, and it is clear why the iPad can stylishly fulfill all of your computing needs.

Simplicity of the iPad

Computers have become a central part of our everyday lives, but there is no reason why they need to be complex devices that have us scratching our heads as to how to best use them. The iPad is not only stylish and compact; it also makes the computing process as simple as possible, so you can concentrate on what you want to do. Some ways in which this is done are:

- **Quickly on**. With the iPad there is no long wait for it to turn on, or wake from a state of sleep. When you turn it on, it is ready to use; it's as simple as that.

- **Apps**. iPad apps sit on the Home screen, visible and ready to use. Most apps are created in a similar format, so once you have mastered getting around them you will be comfortable using most apps.

- **Settings**. One of the built-in iPad apps is Settings. This is a one-stop shop for customizing the way that your iPad looks and operates, and also how settings for apps work.

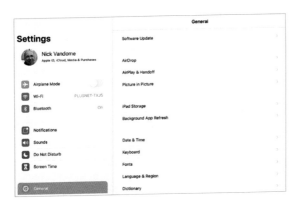

- **Dock and App Switcher window**. These are two functions that enable you to access your favorite apps quickly, regardless of what you are doing on your iPad.

- **Home button**. This enables you to return to the main Home screen at any time. It also has some additional functionality, depending on how many times you click it.

Hot tip

Much of the way you navigate around the iPad is done by tapping or swiping with your fingers, rather than with a traditional keyboard and mouse. There is also a virtual keyboard for input functions.

9

Don't forget

The Dock is the bar at the bottom of the iPad screen, onto which apps can be placed for quick access.

Models and Sizes

Since its introduction in 2010, the iPad has evolved in both its size and specifications. It is now a family of devices, rather than a single size. When choosing your iPad, the first consideration is which size to select. There are four options:

- **iPad**. This is the original version of the iPad, and retains the standard iPad title. Its high-resolution Retina Display screen measures 10.2 inches (diagonal). At the time of printing, the latest version is the 8th generation of the standard-size iPads and supports using the Apple Pencil and the Smart Keyboard (bought separately – see pages 12-13 for more details). The Smart Keyboard has a Smart Connector to attach it and this ensures it works as soon as it is attached. The Apple Pencil has to be "paired" with the iPad, which involves opening **Settings > Bluetooth** and turning Bluetooth **On**. Then, attach the Apple Pencil via the Lightning Connector. It should then be paired and ready for use.

- **iPad Air**. This is similar to the standard iPad, but with a 10.9-inch display. However, it is the thinnest of the iPad models, at 6.1 mm, and supports use of the Apple Pencil and the Smart Keyboard.

- **iPad mini**. The iPad mini is similar in most respects to the larger version, including the Retina Display screen, except for its size. The screen is 7.9 inches (diagonal) and it is also slightly lighter. The latest version, at the time of printing, is the 5th-generation iPad mini and it supports use of the Apple Pencil.

- **iPad Pro**. This is a powerful all-round iPad. It comes with either an 11- or a 12.9-inch screen. It can be used with the Apple Pencil and the Smart Keyboard and is ideal for productivity tasks.

Don't forget

Another variation in the iPad family is how they connect to the internet and online services. This is either with just Wi-Fi connectivity or Wi-Fi and 5G/4G connectivity (where available, but it also covers 3G). This should be considered if you will need to connect to the internet with a cellular connection when you are traveling away from home. 5G, 4G and 3G enable you to connect to a mobile network to access the internet, in the same way as with a cell/mobile phone. This requires a contract with a provider of this type of service.

Specifications Explained

Most models of iPad have the same range of specifications (the main difference being the screen sizes). Some of the specifications to consider are:

- **Processor**: This determines the speed at which the iPad operates and how quickly tasks are performed.

- **Storage**: This determines how much content can be stored on the iPad. Across the iPad family, the range is 32 gigabytes (GB), 64GB, 128GB, 256GB, 512GB or 1 terabyte (TB).

- **Connectivity**: The options for this are Wi-Fi and 5G/4G/3G connectivity for the internet, and Bluetooth for connecting to other devices over short distances.

- **Cameras**: The front-facing camera is a FaceTime one, which is best for video calls or "selfies" (self-portraits). The back-facing camera is a high-resolution one that takes excellent photos and videos.

- **Screen**: iPads that can run iPadOS 14 all have Retina Display screens for the highest resolution and best clarity. This is an LED-backlit screen.

- **Operating system**: The latest version of the iPad operating system is iPadOS 14.

- **Battery power**: This is the length of time the iPad can be used for general use, such as surfing the web on Wi-Fi, watching video, or listening to music. All models offer approximately 10 hours of use in this way.

- **Input/Output**: These include a Lightning Connector port (for charging), 3.5 mm stereo headphone minijack, built-in speaker, microphone and nano-SIM card tray (Wi-Fi and 5G/4G/3G model only).

- **Sensors**: These are used to determine the amount of ambient light and also the orientation in which the iPad is being held. The sensors include an accelerometer, ambient light sensor, barometer and gyroscope.

The amount of storage you need may change once you have bought your iPad. If possible, buy a version with as much as possible, as you cannot add more later.

The main camera on the iPad and the iPad mini is 8 megapixels. On the iPad Pro 11-inch and 12.9-inch, and the iPad Air (4th generation), it is 12 megapixels.

Some models of the iPad Pro (2018 and later) and the iPad Air (4th generation) have a USB-C Connector, rather than a Lightning Connector. This is used for charging the iPad and it can also be used to connect a USB-C flashdrive – see page 70 for details.

The Apple Pencil has been updated in iPadOS 14 to make it easier to write on the screen, and there is also an updated set of options for editing text (see pages 88-89 for details).

Hot tip

The Apple Pencil can be used to annotate PDF documents or screenshots simply by writing on them. This is known as Instant Markup. To annotate a screenshot, press and hold the **On/Off** button and **Home** button simultaneously to capture the screenshot. A thumbnail of the screenshot appears in the bottom left-hand corner for a few seconds. Tap once on this to expand it, and use the drawing tools at the bottom of the screen to annotate it. The annotated image can then be saved into the Photos app.

Apple Pencil

The Apple Pencil is a stylus that can be used on the screen instead of your finger to perform a variety of tasks. At the time of printing, it can be used with all of the iPad models. It can be used for the following:

- Drawing intricate (or simple) artwork using drawing or painting apps.

- Moving around web pages by swiping or tapping on links to access other web pages.

- Selecting items of text by tapping on them and also dragging the selection handles.

- Annotating PDF documents.

Charging the Apple Pencil

The Apple Pencil can be charged using the iPad Lightning Connector port (the same one as for charging the iPad) or the iPad's charging cable, using the Apple Pencil's Lightning adapter, which is supplied with the Apple Pencil.

To check the level of Apple Pencil charge, swipe from left to right on the Home screen to access Today View (see page 34) and swipe down to the **Batteries** section (and also view the level of charge for the iPad).

	iPad	22%
	Apple Pencil	57%

Smart Keyboard

Although the virtual keyboard on the iPad (see Chapter 4 for details) is excellent for text and data inputting or shorter pieces of writing, it is not ideal for longer tasks such as writing a vacation journal or a family history. To overcome this, the Apple Smart Keyboard has been introduced and can be used on all iPad models except the iPad mini. It is a fully-functioning external keyboard that also doubles as a cover. The Smart Keyboard is connected with the Smart Connector that matches the one on the body of the iPad.

Smart Keyboard Shortcuts bar

When typing with the Smart Keyboard, the same Shortcuts bar is available as with the virtual keyboard, specific to the current app.

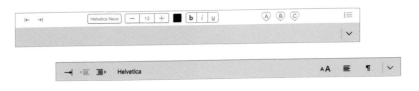

Tap on an item on the Shortcuts bar to access it.

Smart Keyboard shortcuts

Some of the keyboard shortcuts that can be performed on the Smart Keyboard are:

- **Command (cmd) + H** – return to Home screen.

- **Command + Tab** – access the App Switcher bar, in the middle of the screen. Press the Tab button to move through the apps in the App Switcher. Stop at the app you want to open.

- **Command + spacebar** – access the Spotlight Search.

- **Press and hold Command** – a list of Smart Keyboard shortcuts in specific apps.

- **Globe key** – access available keyboards, including the emoji keyboard for adding emoji icons to text.

Don't forget

If a Smart Keyboard is not used, the virtual one will be available instead.

Hot tip

The Smart Keyboard also supports standard keyboard shortcuts such as:

Command + C: Copy.

Command + V: Paste.

Command + X: Cut.

Command + Z: Undo.

Command + B: Adds bold to selected text.

Command + I: Adds italics to selected text.

Command + U: Adds underline to selected text.

To turn on the iPad, press and hold the **On/Off** button for a few seconds. It can also be used to Sleep the iPad or Wake it from the Sleep state, by pressing it once.

Hot tip

The latest version of the iPad Air (4th generation) uses the top button on the body of the iPad to perform the functions of the Home button.

14

Hot tip

If your iPad ever freezes, or if something is not working properly, it can be rebooted by holding down the **Home** button and the **On/Off** button for 10 seconds and then turning it on again by pressing and holding the **On/Off** button.

Before you Switch On

The external controls for the iPad are simple. Three of them are situated at the top of the iPad and the other is in the middle, at the bottom. There are also two cameras, one on the front and one on the back of the iPad.

Controls

The controls at the top of the iPad are:

On/Off button.

Cameras. One is located on the back, underneath the On/Off button and one on the front, at the top.

Volume Up and **Down** buttons.

Home button. Press this once to wake up the iPad or return to the Home screen at any point.

Speakers. The speakers are located on the bottom edge of the iPad.

Lightning Connector. Connect the Lightning Connector here to charge the iPad, or connect it to another computer. Some models of the iPad Pro (2018 and later) and the iPad Air (4th generation) use a USB-C Connector rather than a Lightning Connector. This means it can also be used with a USB-C flashdrive – see page 70 for details.

Getting Started

To start using the iPad, hold down the On/Off button for a few seconds. Initially, there will be a series of setup screens:

- **Language** and **Country**. Select a language and country.

- **Quick Start**. This can be used to transfer settings from another compatible iOS device, such as an iPhone.

- **Wi-Fi network**. Connect to the internet, using either your own home network or a public Wi-Fi hotspot.

- **Data & Privacy**. This is used to identify features that ask for your personal information.

- **Touch ID**. Use this on compatible models to create a Touch ID for unlocking your iPad with a fingerprint.

- **Create a Passcode**. This can be used to create a numerical passcode for unlocking your iPad.

- **Apps & Data**. This can be used to set up an iPad from an iCloud backup, or as a new iPad.

- **Apple ID and iCloud**. This can be used to use an existing iCloud account or create a new one.

- **Express Settings**. This contains options for specifying how apps manage your data.

- **Keep your iPad Up to Date**. This can be used to install updates to the operating system (iOS) automatically.

- **Siri**. This is used to set up Siri, the digital voice assistant.

- **Screen Time**. This can be used to set limits for using apps on the iPad and for creating a usage report.

- **App Analytics**. This can allow details from the iPad and its apps to be sent to Apple and developers.

- **True Tone Display**. This automatically ensures that the screen adapts to the current lighting conditions.

- **Appearance**. This can be used to select Dark or Light mode for the overall appearance on the iPad.

A lot of the initial settings can be skipped during the setup process and accessed later from the **Settings** app.

For details about obtaining an Apple ID, see page 105.

For more information about using iCloud, see pages 64-66.

At the end of the setup process there are three screens detailing the methods for accessing the Dock, the App Switcher for recently-used apps, and the Control Center.

iPadOS 14 is the latest operating system for the iPad.

iPadOS 14 is not compatible with some older models of iPad but can be run on: iPad mini 4 and later; iPad 5th generation and later; iPad Air 2 and later; and all models of iPad Pro. The iPad model number is on the back of the iPad – visit **https://support.apple. com/en-us/HT201471** to find out which model you have.

To check the version of iPadOS, look in **Settings** > **General** > **Software Update**.

About iPadOS 14

iPadOS 14 is the second version of the iPad operating system that is a separate version to the one used on both iPads and iPhones, iOS. However, although iPadOS 14 has its own designation, it is still very closely aligned to the latest version of iOS (iOS 14). Where iPadOS 14 differs from iOS is in the iPad-specific features, such as enhanced multitasking options and some keyboard enhancements. Some of the new features in iPadOS 14 include:

- **Today View panel**. The Today View panel, which can be accessed from the Home screen by swiping to the right from the left-hand edge of the screen, has been redesigned so that the widgets within it can be edited and also displayed at different sizes. Apps can also be included within a Smart Stack, which can display the most relevant items at different times of the day – e.g. the Weather app.

- **App menus**. The built-in apps for the iPad have been standardized as much as possible in iPadOS 14, in terms of their menu structure. Sidebars can be shown or hidden by tapping once on this button, and this feature is available in the Calendar, Contacts, Files, Mail, Music, Notes, Photos, Shortcuts, and Voice Memos apps.

- **Using the Apple Pencil**. The functionality for using the Apple Pencil with the iPad has been expanded with iPadOS 14. Handwritten notes can be converted into typed text, and items can be deleted and selected using the Apple Pencil.

- **Compact calls**. When you receive a FaceTime call on your iPad, or a call from an iPhone, it is displayed in a banner at the top of the screen, rather than taking up the whole display.

- **Updated apps**. A number of iPad apps have been updated in iPadOS 14, including Maps, Messages, Notes, Safari, and Home.

Home Screen

Once you have completed the setup process, you will see the Home screen of the iPad. This contains the built-in apps:

At the bottom of the screen are five apps that appear by default in the Dock area (left-hand side) and recently-accessed apps (right-hand side).

Rotate the iPad, and the orientation changes automatically.

There are 38 different default wallpaper backgrounds for iPadOS 14 on the iPad. These can be found in **Settings > Wallpaper**. The options are: **Dynamic**, which means that they appear to move independently from the app icons when you tilt the iPad; and **Stills**, which are static images; and you can also use your own pictures from the Photos app.

Items on the Dock can be removed and new ones can be added. For more details, see pages 26-27.

Home Button

The Home button, located at the bottom-middle of the iPad, can be used to perform a number of tasks:

The latest version of the iPad Air (4th generation) uses the top button on the body of the iPad to perform the functions of the Home button.

Don't forget

For more details about the App Switcher, see page 28.

1 Click once on the **Home** button to return to the Home screen at any point

2 Double-click on the **Home** button to access the **App Switcher** window. This shows the most recently-used and open apps

Hot tip

Pinch together with thumb and four fingers on the screen to return to the Home screen from any open app.

3 Press and hold on the **Home** button to access Siri, the voice assistant function

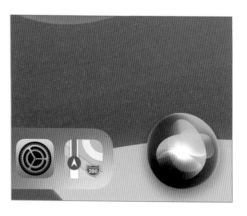

Don't forget

For more information about using the iPad search facilities, see pages 50-51.

Opening Items

All apps on your iPad can be opened with minimum fuss and effort:

1 Tap once on an icon to open the app

2 The app opens at its own Home screen

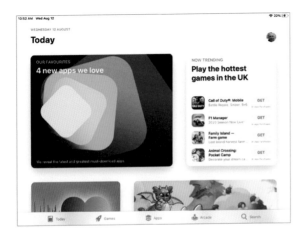

For details about using the App Switcher, and closing items, see pages 28-29.

3 Click once on the **Home** button to return to the main iPad Home screen

4 From the App Switcher window, swipe between apps and tap on one to open it directly

The screen can also be locked by pressing once on the **On/Off** button.

Notifications can be displayed on the iPad's Lock screen. This can be activated by going to **Settings** > **Notifications** > **Show Previews** and then selecting **Always**.

Once the passcode has been set, tap on the **Require Passcode** button in the Touch ID & Passcode section to specify when the passcode is activated. The best option is **Immediately**, otherwise someone else could access your iPad before the passcode is activated.

Using the Lock Screen

To save power, it is possible to set your iPad screen to lock automatically. This is the equivalent of the Sleep option on a traditional computer. To do this:

1 Tap once on the **Settings** app

2 Tap once on the **Display & Brightness** tab

3 Tap once on the **Auto-Lock** option

4 Select a length of time until the iPad is locked automatically, when it is not being used

Locking and unlocking an iPad

When the iPad is locked – i.e. the Lock screen is displayed – it can be unlocked simply by pressing the **Home** button. However, this is not secure, as anyone could unlock the iPad. A better option is to add a numerical passcode. To do this:

1 Select **Settings** > **Touch ID & Passcode**

2 Tap once on the **Turn Passcode On** button

3 Enter a 6-digit passcode. This can be used to unlock your iPad from the Lock screen. Confirm the passcode on the next screen. The passcode is now required on the Lock screen whenever the iPad is locked

Fingerprint sensor with Touch ID

For greater security, the Home button can be used as a fingerprint sensor to unlock your iPad with the unique fingerprint that has set it up. (A passcode also has to be set up in case the Touch ID does not work.) To do this:

1 Select **Settings > Touch ID & Passcode**

2 Create a passcode as shown on the previous page (this is required if the fingerprint sensor is unavailable for any reason).
Drag the **iPad Unlock** button **On**

3 Tap once on the **Add a Fingerprint...** link. This presents a screen for creating your Touch ID

4 Place your finger on the **Home** button several times to create the Touch ID. This will include capturing the edges of your finger. The screens move automatically after each part is captured, and the fingerprint icon turns red. Complete the Touch ID wizard to
create a unique fingerprint for unlocking your iPad

Place Your Finger

Lift and rest your finger on the Home button repeatedly.

Hot tip

A Touch ID and passcode can be used to set up Apple Pay, to be used for paying for items on the web. For more details, see page 128.

Don't forget

The fingerprint sensor is very effective, although it may take a bit of practice until you can get the right position for your finger to unlock the iPad first time, every time. It can only be unlocked with the same finger that created the Touch ID in Step 4. Additional fingerprints can also be set up. The Touch ID may not work if your finger is wet.

Charging your iPad

The iPad comes with a Lightning Connector to USB cable and a USB power adapter, for charging the iPad:

Don't forget

iPads that can run iPadOS 14 have Lightning Connectors; or the newer USB-C Connector that is available on the iPad Pro, 2018 and later.

1 Connect the USB end of the Lightning Connector to the power adapter

2 Connect the other end of the Lightning Connector to the iPad

Hot tip

If you have older accessories with Dock connector points, you can buy a Lightning to 30-pin adapter so that you can still use them with a 4th-generation (and later) iPad.

3 Plug in the power adapter

The iPad can also be charged by connecting it with the Lightning Connector to another computer.

2 Around your iPad

Once you have turned on your iPad you will want to start using it as soon as possible. This chapter shows how to do this, with details about settings; navigation; using the Today View panel; accessibility features; the digital voice assistant, Siri; and using Screen Time to monitor the usage of your iPad.

Don't forget

If a Settings option has an **On/Off** button next to it, this can be changed by swiping the button to either the left or right. Green indicates that the option is **On**.

Hot tip

The Display & Brightness setting has an option for Dark Mode, which inverts the screen, with a dark background and white text. This can make the screen easier to read in certain conditions. To use Dark Mode, tap **On** the **Dark** button. To specify when Dark Mode is activated drag the **Automatic** button **On**, or tap once on the **Options** button to specify a time for Dark Mode.

iPad Settings

The Settings app controls settings for the appearance of the iPad and the way it and its apps operate:

- **Apple ID and iCloud**. This contains settings for items that are to be saved to the online iCloud service (see pages 64-66).

- **Airplane Mode**. This can be used while on an airplane.

- **Wi-Fi**. This enables you to select a wireless network.

- **Bluetooth**. Turn this **On** to connect Bluetooth devices.

- **Notifications**. This determines how the Notification Center operates (see pages 142-143).

- **Sounds**. This has options for setting sounds for alerts.

- **Do Not Disturb**. Use this to specify times when you do not want to receive audio alerts or FaceTime video calls.

- **Screen Time**. This is used to view details of your iPad use and add restrictions (see pages 52-56).

- **General**. This contains a number of options for how the iPad operates. This is one of the most useful settings.

- **Control Center**. This determines how the Control Center operates (see pages 30-33).

- **Display & Brightness**. This can be used to set the screen brightness, text size and bold text.

- **Home Screen & Dock**. This has an option for the size of the Home screen icons and also displaying Today View on the Home screen.

- **Accessibility**. This can be used for users with visual or motor issues (see pages 58-62 for details).

- **Wallpaper**. To change the iPad's wallpaper, tap once on the **Choose a New Wallpaper** option.

- **Siri & Search**. Options for turning on the digital voice assistant, and settings such as language and voice style.

- **Apple Pencil**. This has options for using an Apple Pencil with an iPad.

- **Touch ID & Passcode**. This has options for creating a unique fingerprint ID for unlocking your iPad (see page 21) and also using Apple Pay (see page 128).

- **Battery**. This shows the battery usage of specific apps and can show the battery level in the status bar.

- **Privacy**. This can be used to activate Location Services so that your location can be used by specific apps.

- **App Store**. This can be used to specify download options for the App Store.

- **Wallet & Apple Pay**. This can be used to set up Apple Pay for online payments (see page 128 for details).

- **Passwords**. This contains options for managing website passwords.

- **Mail, Contacts, Calendars**. These are three separate settings, with options for how these three apps operate.

iPad app settings

Most of the built-in iPad apps have their own settings that determine how the apps operate. These include: Notes, Reminders, Voice Memos, Messages, FaceTime, Maps, Measure, Safari,

News, Stocks, Home, Shortcuts, Music, TV, Photos, Camera, Books, and Podcasts. Tap on one of these tabs to view the settings for that app. (Apps that are downloaded from the App Store also have their individual settings in this location in the Settings app.)

If you have an iPad with 5G/4G/3G connectivity, there will also be a setting for Cellular/Mobile.

Tap the arrow to see additional options:

Tap once here to move back to the previous page for the selected setting:

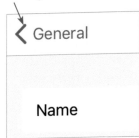

Using the Dock

The Dock is an element that has been part of the iPad since it was introduced. The Dock has two separate sections: the standard Dock area for your most frequently-used apps; and a section for recently-used apps, or those open on another Apple device using iPadOS, iOS or macOS. The icons that are displayed change as different apps are accessed on the iPad, or on the other device.

Elements of the Dock

Standard apps (by default, these are Messages, Safari, Music, Mail, and Files) are displayed on the left-hand side.

Dynamic items that change each time a new app is opened, or certain apps opened on another Apple device using iPadOS, iOS or macOS are displayed on the right-hand side.

If a compatible app is open on another Apple device – e.g. an iPhone – this label appears in the right-hand corner. Tap on the app to open the same item as it is displaying on the other

Apple device. Apps that operate in this way are those linked through iCloud, and include the web browser Safari, Mail, Messages, Reminders, Calendar, Contacts, and Notes.

Hot tip

Just above the Dock is a line of small dots. These indicate how many Home screens of content there are on the iPad. Tap on one of the dots to go to that Home screen, or swipe to the left or right to move between them. The white dot indicates the position of the current Home screen being viewed.

Don't forget

The functionality of open apps on other Apple devices is known as **Handoff** and can be turned On or Off in **Settings** > **General** > **AirPlay & Handoff**.

…

...cont'd

Adding and removing Dock items

The default items on the Dock can be removed and other apps added, as required. To do this:

1 Press on an item on the Dock and drag it onto the main area of the Home screen

2 Repeat the process for an app on the Home screen to drag it onto the Dock

Accessing the Dock

The Dock can also be accessed from any app, not just from the Home screen. To do this:

1 From within any app, use a short swipe up from the bottom of the screen to access the Dock

Don't forget

Up to 12 apps can be added to the left-hand side of the Dock. However, this reduces the size at which the apps' icons appear. There are only ever three items on the right-hand side of the Dock, and this changes each time a new app is opened or accessed (unless it is already in the main area of the Dock).

27

Hot tip

Press the **Home** button once to return to the Home screen, displaying the Dock, from any app.

App Switcher Window

The App Switcher feature in iPadOS 14 performs a number of shortcuts and useful tasks:

● It shows open apps and enables you to move between these and access them by tapping once on the required item.

● It enables apps to be closed (see next page).

Accessing App Switcher

The App Switcher window can be accessed from any screen on your iPad, as follows:

(see next page)

Don't forget

Press the **Home** button once to exit the App Switcher and return to the app you were using immediately before accessing the App Switcher.

Hot tip

Swipe up from the bottom of the screen slightly further than the middle of the screen to return to the Home screen, rather than the App Switcher.

1 Double-click on the **Home** button, or

2 Swipe up from the bottom of any screen. This should be a long swipe, up to the middle of the screen at least. A short swipe will bring up the Dock at the bottom of the screen, rather than the App Switcher

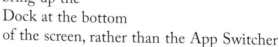

3 Tap on an app in the App Switcher to make it the active one

28

Closing Items

The iPad deals with open apps very efficiently. They rarely interact with other apps, which increases security and also means that they can be open in the background, without using up a significant amount of processing power, in a state of semi-hibernation until they are needed. Because of this, it is not essential to close apps when you move to something else. However, you may want to close apps if you feel you have too many open or if one stops working. To do this:

Don't forget

When you switch from one app to another, the first one stays open in the background. You can go back to it by accessing it from the App Switcher window or the Home screen.

1 Access the App Switcher window. The currently-open apps are displayed

2 Press and hold on an app and swipe it to the top of the screen to close it. This does not remove it from the iPad and it can be opened again in the usual way

Don't forget

Swipe left and right in the App Switcher window to view all of the open apps.

3 The app is removed from its position in the App Switcher window and the other apps move to fill the space

Using the Control Center

The Control Center is a panel containing commonly-used options within the **Settings** app, and is an excellent option for when you do not want to have to go into Settings.

Accessing the Control Center

The Control Center can be accessed from any screen within iPadOS 14, and it can also be accessed from the Lock screen:

1 Swipe down from the top right-hand corner of the Home screen, or any app, or the Lock screen, to access the Control Center panel

Control Center functionality

The Control Center contains items that have differing formats and functionality. To access these:

1 Press on the folder of four icons to access the **Airplane Mode**, **AirDrop**, **Wi-Fi** and **Bluetooth** options

Don't forget

AirDrop is the functionality for sharing items wirelessly between compatible devices. Tap once on the **AirDrop** button in the Control Center and specify whether you want to share with **Contacts Only** or **Everyone**. Once AirDrop is set up, you can use the **Share** button in compatible apps to share items such as photos with any other AirDrop users in the vicinity.

2 Press on the **Music** button to expand the options for music controls, including playing or pausing items and changing the volume. Tap once on this icon to send music from your iPad to other compatible devices, such as AirPod earphones or HomePods (Apple's wireless speakers)

3 Tap once on individual buttons to turn items On or Off (they change color depending on their state)

4 Drag on these items to increase or decrease the screen brightness and the volume

When **Airplane Mode** is activated in the second Step 1 on the previous page, the network and wireless connectivity on the iPad is disabled. However, it can still be used for functions such as playing music or reading books, as long as they have been downloaded to the iPad.

Press on the brightness and volume buttons to access panels that allow greater precision by dragging on their respective bars.

31

32

...cont'd

Control Center options
Items in the Control Center can be accessed as follows:

Press on the **Flashlight** button to access bars for the strength of the flashlight. Drag on the bars to alter the level of the flashlight.

- Tap once on this button to turn **Airplane Mode** On or Off.

- Tap once on this button to activate **AirDrop** for sharing items with other AirDrop users.

- Tap once on this button to turn **Wi-Fi** On or Off.

- Tap once on this button to turn **Bluetooth** On or Off.

- Tap once on this button to **Lock** or **Unlock** screen rotation. If it is locked, the screen will not change when you change the orientation of your iPad.

- Tap once on this button to **Mute** all sounds.

- Tap once on this button to turn **Do Not Disturb** mode On or Off.

- Tap once on this button to turn On the **Flashlight**. Press on the button to access the option to change the brightness (see tip).

- Tap once on this button to open the **Camera** app. Press on the button to access options for taking a selfie (a self-portrait), recording a video, recording a slow-motion video and taking a standard photo.

Customizing the Control Center

The items in the Control Center can be customized so that items can be added or removed. To do this:

1 Tap once on the **Settings** app

2 Tap once on the **Control Center** tab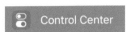

3 The items currently in the Control Center are shown at the top of the window; those that can be added are below them. Tap once on a red icon to remove an existing item, or tap once on a green icon to add new items to the Control Center

4 Items that are added in Step 3 are included in the Control Center, and can be accessed from here

Dark Mode, for changing the screen background and text color, can also be added to the Control Center, from the list in Step 3.

The Control Center also has a Screen Mirroring option, for displaying what is on the iPad on a compatible High-Definition TV.

33

Today View Panel

The Today View panel can be used to display information from some of your favorite and most-used apps. It can also be pinned to the Home screen so that it is always visible there. To use the Today View panel:

1 Swipe from left to right on the left-hand edge of the Home screen to access the Today View panel, which contains the Today View widgets

Swipe from right to left on the Today View panel to hide it from the Home screen, unless it has been pinned there (see next page).

2 Swipe up on the Today View panel to see all of the widgets currently in it. Tap on a widget to open it in its related app

3 Press and hold anywhere within the Today View panel to access its editing controls

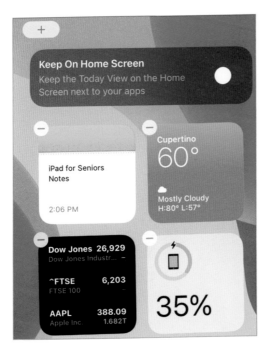

Hot tip

Widgets can also be removed from the Today View panel by pressing and holding on a widget within the panel. Tap once on the **Remove Widget** button and tap once on the **Remove** button.

35

4 Tap once on this icon in the top left-hand corner of a widget and tap once on the **Remove** button to remove it from the Today View panel

Remove "Weather"?

Cancel   Remove

Hot tip

The Today View panel can also be assigned to remain on the Home screen from **Settings** > **Home Screen & Dock** and by dragging the **Keep Today View on Home Screen** button **On**.

5 At the top of the Today View panel, drag the **Keep On Home Screen** button **On** to pin the Today View panel on the Home screen

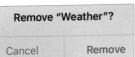

Today View Widgets

The iPadOS widgets can be added to the Today View panel and some of them can also be edited to change their functionality.

Adding widgets
To add widgets to the Today View panel:

The widgets in the Today View panel have been updated in iPadOS 14.

1 Press and hold anywhere within the Today View panel and tap once on this button at the top of the Today View panel

2 The Today View widgets are displayed

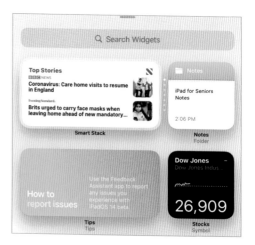

3 Swipe up the panel to view the full list of available widgets

4 Tap once on a widget to view options for adding it to the Today View panel

Being able to select widgets at different sizes is a new feature in iPadOS 14.

5 Swipe from right to left, or tap on the dots toward the bottom of the window, to access the different sizes at which the widget can be used. The sizes are small, medium or large

Hot tip

Several instances of the same widget can be added to the Today View panel. This can be useful if the widget is editable and so multiple instances can display different information. For instance, if you add several versions of the Weather widget, they can all display weather forecasts from different locations.

6 Tap once on the **Add Widget** button

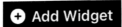

7 The widget is added to the Today View panel, at the size selected in Step 5

...cont'd

Editing widgets

Some of the widgets in the Today View panel can be edited within the panel. The widgets with this functionality include: Calendar; News; Notes; Reminders; Stocks; and Weather. To edit a widget in the Today View panel:

Editable widgets in the Today View panel is a new feature in iPadOS 14.

1 Press and hold on a widget within the Today View panel and tap once on the **Edit Widget** button (if available)

2 Edit the widget as required. For instance, for the Weather widget, tap once on the **Location** button

3 Select a new location, or search for one using the Search box at the top of the window

4 The new location is displayed by the Weather widget

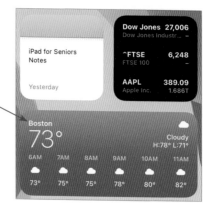

Moving widgets

The widgets in the Today View panel can be moved around, so you can order the panel exactly how you want. To do this:

1 Press and hold on a widget in the Today View panel until the Today View controls appear

Beware

Widgets cannot be placed within another widget: if they are moved over another widget, it will move aside to accommodate the first widget.

2 Drag the widget into a new position. Widgets remain at their selected sizes and other widgets will be reordered to accommodate the moved widget accordingly

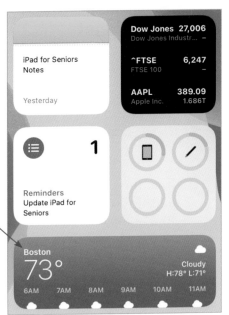

...cont'd

Smart Stack widgets

Since the amount of space in the Today View panel is limited, it is important to have as much information in each widget as possible. This is where Smart Stack widgets come into their own. Smart Stacks are widgets that contain several elements – e.g. Photos, News, Calendar and Notes. Each item can be scrolled through within the Smart Stack widget. To use Smart Stacks:

Smart Stack widgets in the Today View panel is a new feature in iPadOS 14.

1 Press and hold anywhere within the Today View panel and tap once on this button at the top of the Today View panel

2 In the widgets window, tap once on the **Smart Stack** widget

3 Select the required size for the Smart Stack and tap once on the **Add Widget** button

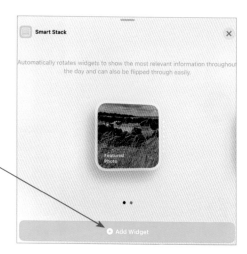

Don't forget

Swipe left or right on the app's icon in Step 3 to select the size for the Smart Stack.

4 The Smart Stack widget is added to the Today View panel. The number of elements in the Smart Stack widget is indicated by the dots to the right of the widget. Swipe up on the Smart Stack to view the different items

Editing a Smart Stack widget

Once a Smart Stack has been added to the Today View panel it can be edited in various ways:

1 Press and hold on a Smart Stack widget. Tap on one of the editing options, which can be for the selected widget within the Smart Stack, or the Stack itself

Edit "Calendar"	ⓘ
Remove "Calendar"	🗂
Edit Stack	⬜
Remove Stack	⊖

2 The items within the Smart Stack are displayed. Drag the **Smart Rotate** button **On** to enable the items within the Smart Stack to be displayed in the correct way for viewing

Don't forget

Swipe from right to left on a widget in Step 2 and tap once on the **Delete** button to remove it from the Smart Stack.

Delete

3 Press and hold here and drag an item to change its order within the Smart Stack

Navigating Around

Much of the navigation on the iPad is done with Multitasking Gestures, which are combinations of tapping, swiping and pinching gestures that can be used to view items such as web pages, photos, maps and documents.

Swiping between screens

Once you have added more apps to your iPad, they will start to fill up more screens. To move between these, swipe left or right with one or two fingers.

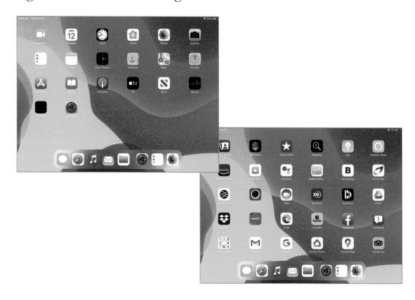

You can also move between different screens by tapping once on one of the small white dots in the middle of the screen above the Dock.

You can also return to the Home screen by clicking once on the **Home** button.

Returning to the Home screen

Pinch together with thumb and four fingers to return to the Home screen from any open app, or swipe up from the bottom of the screen. The Home screen can also be accessed by using a long swipe up from the bottom of any screen (a short swipe brings up the Dock, and a slightly longer one brings up the App Switcher).

Swiping up and down

Swipe up and down with one finger to move up or down web pages, photos, maps or documents. The content moves in the opposite direction of the swipe; i.e. if you swipe up, the page will move down, and vice versa.

The faster you swipe on the screen, the faster the screen moves up or down.

Tapping and zooming

Double-tap with one finger to zoom in on a web page, photo, map or document. Double-tap with one finger to return to the original view.

Pinching and swiping

Swipe outwards with thumb and forefinger to zoom in on a web page, photo, map or document.

Pinch together with thumb and forefinger to zoom back out on a web page, photo, map or document.

Swiping outwards with thumb and forefinger enables you to zoom in on an item to a greater degree than double-tapping with one finger.

More Gestures

- Swipe left or right with four or five fingers to move between open apps.

- Drag with two or three fingers to move a web page, photo, map or document.

- Press and swipe down on any free area on the Home screen to access the Spotlight Search box.

- Swipe left or right with one finger to move between full-size photos in the Photos app.

- Tap once on a photo thumbnail with one finger to enlarge it to full screen within the Photos app.

- Drag down from the top right-hand corner of any screen to access the Control Center.

- Drag down at the top-middle of the iPad to view current notifications in the Notification Center.

The Multitasking Gestures involving four or five fingers can be turned On or Off in the **General** section of the **Settings** app (**Settings** > **Home Screen & Dock** > **Multitasking**).

Slide Over

The iPad has evolved from being an internet-enabled communication and entertainment device into something that is now a genuine productivity device. With iPadOS 14, productivity options are enhanced with the use of Slide Over and Split View (only with certain models of iPad). These are options that enable two apps to be viewed and worked with, within a single screen. This means it is much easier to perform several tasks without having to constantly switch between apps.

Slide Over is an option that is available on the iPad, iPad Pro, iPad mini 2 (and later), and iPad Air (and later). It enables you to activate a second app as a floating bar while another app is open at full screen below it. To do this:

Hot tip

For apps that you will use regularly in Slide Over and Split View, add them to the main area of the Dock so that they are always available in Step 3.

Don't forget

Use a short swipe up from the bottom of the screen to access the Dock.

1 Open the first app that you want to use

2 Swipe up from the bottom of the screen to access the Dock

3 Press and hold on an app on the Dock and drag it over the first app

4 Release the second app. It will snap to the left- or right-hand side of the screen as a floating bar over the first app

5 Press and hold on this button to drag the Slide Over panel to either side of the screen (or swipe on the button, from right to left)

6 The two apps can be used independently of each other; e.g. move through different views in Photos and then move through your Twitter feed

Don't forget

If the main app is exited – e.g. by going back to the Home screen – the Slide Over panel will still be available when you access the main app again, by swiping inwards from the right-hand edge of the screen.

...cont'd

Multiple apps in Slide Over

Slide Over view can not only display a single app; it can also be used to add several apps within the Slide Over panel, so that they can be accessed quickly in this mode. To do this:

1 Access Slide Over view, with one app open. Swipe up from the bottom of the screen to access the Dock. Drag another app and release it over the first one to add it to the Slide Over panel

Hot tip

The movement in Step 3 to access all of the apps within the Slide Over panel is a quick flick to the right, rather than a long dragging motion.

2 Repeat the process in Step 1 for all of the apps you want to include within the Slide Over panel

3 On the visible app in Slide Over view, press on the dark bar at the bottom of the app and swipe to the right to reveal the next available app in Slide Over view. Each app can be viewed in this way

4 Press on the dark bar at the bottom of the visible app in Slide Over view and swipe upwards, to show all of the available apps

Hot tip

To enable the use of multiple apps in Slide Over view, ensure that the **Allow Multiple Apps** button is **On** in **Settings** > **Home Screen & Dock** > **Multitasking**.

5 Tap once on an app to make it the currently-active one in Slide Over view

6 Press on an app and swipe it to the top of the window to remove it from Slide Over view

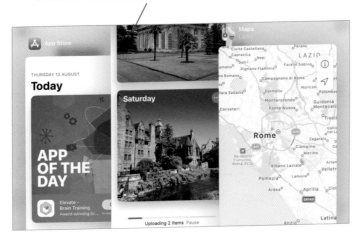

Beware

Not all third-party apps support Split View, but the number is growing.

Hot tip

Several versions of the same app can be displayed in the Split View window. This is known as multiple spaces in Split View. To do this, drag the same app as the current one onto the screen in Step 3.

Hot tip

If more than one version of an app is open in Split View, they can all be viewed by pressing and holding on an app on the Home screen, or the Dock, and tapping once on the **Show All Windows** button. This is known as App Exposé.

Split View

On the iPad, iPad Pro and iPad Air 2 (and later) the concept of Slide Over is taken one step further by Split View: the second item can become fixed, which can then be resized so that it has equal prominence to the first app. To do this:

1 Open the first app that you want to use

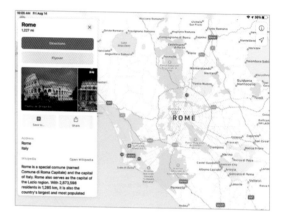

2 Swipe up from the bottom of the screen to access the Dock

3 Press and hold on an app on the Dock and drag it to the right-hand or left-hand side of the screen, and release the app when a dark bar appears below it

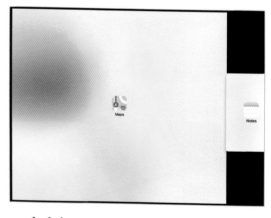

4 Initially, the app in Split View takes up 50% of the screen and can be used independently of the other app

Hot tip

Split View can also be used to copy items between two open, compatible apps, by pressing on them and dragging them into the other app. For instance, a photo can be dragged from the Photos app into an email; text can be highlighted and dragged into the Notes app; and a web link can be highlighted and dragged into another app, so the web page can be accessed from the link. This is known as drag and drop.

5 Drag on the middle button to change the proportions of the two Split View panels

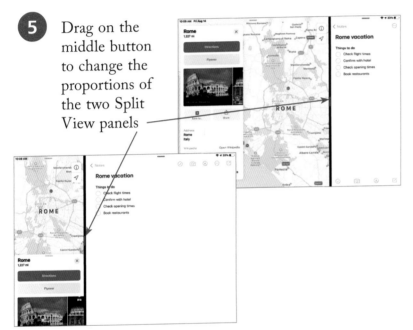

6 Press and hold on the middle button and drag it away from the right-hand (or left-hand) edge of the screen to close one of the Split View apps

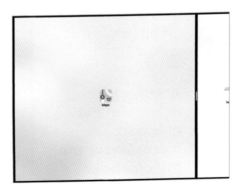

Don't forget

The **Picture in Picture** function enables a FaceTime video, or other video, to be minimized on the screen but remain active so that you can still view it and perform other tasks at the same time.

Finding Things with Siri

Siri is the iPad voice assistant that provides answers to a variety of questions, by looking within your iPad and also with the use of web services. You can ask Siri questions relating to the apps on your iPad, and also general questions such as weather conditions around the world, or sports results. Initially, Siri can be set up within the **Settings** app:

Siri can be used to open any of the built-in iPad apps, simply by saying, for example: "**Open Photos**".

Turn **On** the **Listen for "Hey Siri"** button in the first Step 2 to activate Siri just by saying this phrase, without having to press the **Home** button.

Tap once on this button at the bottom of the screen to ask another question of Siri. The size at which the Siri button is displayed is a new feature in iPadOS 14.

1. Tap once on the **Siri & Search** option

2. Tap once on the options to select a language, set voice feedback, and allow access to your details (Siri can also be set up when you first start to use your iPad)

Questioning Siri

Once you have set up Siri, you can start putting it to work with your queries. To do this:

1. Hold down the **Home** button until the Siri window appears

2. To find something within your iPad apps, make a request such as **Show me my calendar**

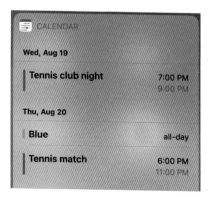

Siri can also find information from across the web and related web services:

1 Siri can provide sports results for certain sports in certain countries, such as in response to the request **Show Red Sox latest score**

2 Global weather reports are another of Siri's strong points, and it can provide forecasts in response to the question **What is the weather like in Athens?**

3 However, even Siri's knowledge is limited and, for some subjects, it will give brief details and a link to Wikipedia or the web instead

Siri can be used with a range of Apple and specific third-party apps. For instance, you can ask it to find specific photos in the Photos app, send a message to someone with the Messages app, and even book restaurants and taxis with compatible apps.

Items can also be searched for using the Spotlight Search option. This can be accessed by swiping downwards on the Home screen and entering a keyword or phrase in the Search box at the top of the window. Items can be searched for on your iPad (including apps), or use the **Search Web** button at the bottom of the window to search the web.

51

Screen Time

The amount of time that we spend on our digital devices is a growing issue in society, and steps are being taken to let us see exactly how much time we are spending looking at our mobile screens. In iPadOS 14, a range of screen-use options can be monitored with the Screen Time feature. To use this:

Hot tip

Once Screen Time has been turned On, it can be turned Off again by tapping once on the **Turn Off Screen Time** button at the bottom of the main Screen Time window.

1 Select **Settings** > **Screen Time**

2 Tap once on the **Turn On Screen Time** button

3 Options for using Screen Time are displayed. Tap once on the **Continue** button

Don't forget

Each week the Screen Time option produces a report based on the overall usage, as shown in Step 5. The report is identified with a notification when it is published each week.

4 Screen Time can be set up for your own use, or on a child's iPad. If it is set up for a child there will be more parental control options for controlling the type of content that is available (see pages 55-56). Tap once on an option

5 The current Screen Time usage is shown at the top of the panel at the right-hand side of the Settings window

Options for Screen Time

On the main Screen Time settings page there are options
for viewing apps and content on your iPad:

1 Tap once on **Downtime**

Downtime
Schedule time away from the screen.

2 Drag the **Downtime**
button **On** and tap once
on the **From** and **To**
buttons to select times
for when only specified
apps are available

〈 Screen Time   **Downtime**

Downtime   ⬤

Set a schedule for time away from the screen. During downtime, only apps that you choose to allow and phone calls will be available.

Every Day   ✓

Customize Days

From   10:00 PM

To   7:00 AM

3 Tap once on **App Limits**

App Limits
Set time limits for apps.

4 Tap once on the
Add Limit
button to add
time limits for
using types
of apps

〈 Screen Time   **App Limits**

Set daily time limits for app categories you want to manage. App limits reset every day at midnight.

Add Limit

5 Select a
category for
the types of
apps that you
want to limit
use of (or select
**All Apps &
Categories**).
Tap once on

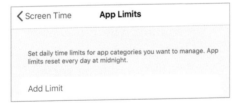

Cancel   **Choose Apps**   Next

MOST USED APPS, CATEGORIES, AND WEBSITES

✓   ≋   All Apps & Categories

✓   💬   Social   All 〉

✓   🎮   Games   All 〉

✓   📺   Entertainment   All 〉

✓   🎨   Creativity   All 〉

✓   📊   Productivity & Finance   All 〉

the **Next** button to specify a time limit for how long
these apps can be used

Don't forget

The time limit for
using apps is only a
suggestion, and the
apps do not stop
operating when
the limit is reached.
Instead, a notification
appears to alert you
to the fact that the
time limit has been
reached. Tap once on
the **Ignore Limit**
button to continue
using the app.

⏳

Time Limit
You've reached your limit on this website.
Ignore Limit

Select an option for
how long you want to
ignore the time limit.

One More Minute

Remind Me in 15 Minutes

Ignore Limit For Today

Cancel

...cont'd

6 Tap once on **Always Allowed**

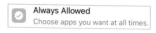

7 The apps that are always allowed to operate, regardless of what settings there are for Screen Time, are displayed. Tap once on the red circle next to one to remove it. Select items below the **Choose Apps** heading to add more

8 Tap once on **Communication Limits**

9 Tap once on **During Screen Time** or **During Downtime** to limit who can contact you, and communicate with you, during these times

10 Tap once on **Content & Privacy Restrictions**

11 Drag the **Content & Privacy Restrictions** button On to apply restrictions for blocking inappropriate content (see next two pages for details)

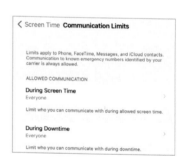

The options for allowing communications in Step 9 are: **Contacts Only**; **Contacts & Groups with at Least One Contact**; or **Everyone**.

Restrictions for Children

If children or grandchildren have access to an iPad, this can raise genuine concerns about the type of content that they may be accessing and also the amount of time that they spend on the device. The Screen Time options can be used to apply specific settings for a child, so that you can have a degree of control over what they are viewing. These are similar to the standard Screen Time options, but they can be set up with an initial selection of wizards, and it is also possible to include a parental passcode that has to be entered when limits are reached. To set up restrictions for children:

In computing terms, a "wizard" is a set of step-by-step instructions that take you through a specific process.

1 Access the Screen Time options as shown on page 52 and tap once on the **This is My Child's iPad** option

This is My iPad

This is My Child's iPad

2 Select options for **Downtime** and **App Limits** as for the standard Screen Time options

3 On the **Content & Privacy** screen, tap once on the **Continue** button

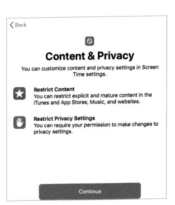

‹ Back

Content & Privacy

You can customize content and privacy settings in Screen Time settings.

Restrict Content
You can restrict explicit and mature content in the iTunes and App Stores, Music, and websites.

Restrict Privacy Settings
You can require your permission to make changes to privacy settings.

Continue

A passcode can also be created for your own Screen Time settings. This prevents anyone from changing these settings and can be used to allow more time once a time limit is reached.

4 Create a parental passcode that will be required to access any restricted content, or override a time limit once it has been reached

‹ Back

Parent Passcode

Create a passcode that will be required to allow for more time, or to make changes to Screen Time settings.

● ● ● ○

...cont'd

Don't forget

In-app purchases involve buying additional items from within an app. Apps that are initially free to download frequently have in-app purchases.

Beware

If apps are disabled in Step 7 they are no longer visible on the iPad's Home screen. To view them, they have to be enabled again in Step 7.

Don't forget

If you are setting restrictions for a child or a grandchild, tell them about it and explain what you are doing and why.

5 Tap once on the **Content & Privacy Restrictions** button, as shown on page 54. Drag the **Content & Privacy Restrictions** button On to access the available options (see page 54)

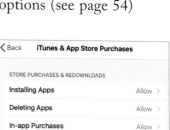

6 Tap once on the **iTunes & App Store Purchases** button in the previous step to set restrictions for installing and deleting apps from the iTunes Store and the App Store and also making in-app purchases

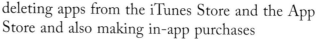

7 Tap once on the **Allowed Apps** button in Step 5 above, and drag the buttons On or Off to enable or disable a specific app

8 Tap once on the **Content Restrictions** button in Step 5 above to select options for parental ratings for movies and TV shows, music, podcasts, books and apps. This determines the type of content that can be accessed from each option

Updating Software

The operating system that powers the iPad is known as iPadOS. This is a mobile-computing operating system that is specifically tailored to the iPad. The latest version is iPadOS 14. Periodically, there are updates to iPadOS to fix bugs and add new features. These can be downloaded to your iPad once they are released:

1. Tap once on the **Settings** app

2. Tap on the **General** tab

3. Tap on the **Software Update** option

Software Update	>

4. If there is an update available (or a new version of iPadOS) it will be displayed here, with details of what is contained within it, from this link

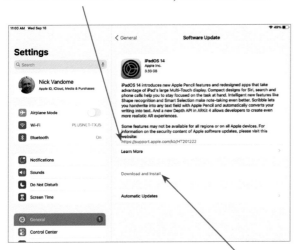

5. Tap once on the **Download and Install** link to start the download process. The iPadOS update will then download and install automatically

If your iPadOS software is up-to-date, there is a message to this effect in the **Software Update** window.

Software Update can be set to be performed automatically overnight, when the iPad is charging and connected to Wi-Fi. Tap on the **Automatic Updates** button in Step 4 and drag the **Automatic Updates** button **On**.

Automatic Updates	

It is always worth updating the iPadOS to keep up-to-date with fixes. Also, app developers update their products to use the latest iPadOS features.

Accessibility Issues

The iPad tries to cater to as wide a range of users as possible, including those who have difficulty with vision or hearing, or those with physical and motor issues. There are a number of settings that can help with these areas. To access the range of accessibility settings:

1 Tap once on the **Settings** app

2 Tap on the **Accessibility** tab

3 The settings for **Vision**, **Physical and Motor**, **Hearing** and **General** are displayed here:

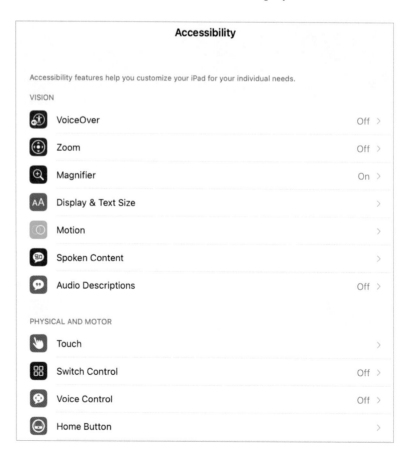

In the Accessibility section, drag the **On/ Off Labels** button **On** to display an extra graphical symbol on the **On/Off** buttons, to further help identify their state.

...cont'd

Vision settings
These can help anyone with impaired vision, and there are options to hear items on the screen and also for making text easier to read:

1 Tap once on the **VoiceOver** option

2 Drag this button **On** to activate the VoiceOver function. This then enables items to be spoken when you tap on them

3 Select options for VoiceOver, as required

VoiceOver works with the built-in iPad apps and some apps from the App Store, but not all of them.

When VoiceOver is On, tap once on an item to select it and have it spoken; double-tap to activate the item.

There is a wide range of options for the way VoiceOver can be used. For full details, see the Apple website at **www.apple.com/accessibility/ios/voiceover**

...cont'd

If you turn on the **Zoom** function, you can magnify areas of the screen with a magnification window. To activate this, double-tap with three fingers. Drag with three fingers within the window to view different areas of the screen, or press and hold on the tab in the middle-bottom of the window to drag it into different positions.

Drag the **LED Flash for Alerts** button **On** in the Audio & Visual window to enable the screen to flash to indicate that an alert or a notification has been received.

4. Tap once on the **Accessibility** button to return to the main options

5. Tap once on these options to access settings for zooming the screen, using a magnifier over the screen and increasing text size

> VISION
>
> VoiceOver
>
> Zoom
>
> Magnifier
>
> AA Display & Text Size

6. Tap again on the **Accessibility** button to return to the main options after each selection

Hearing settings

These can be used to change the iPad speaker from stereo to mono. To do this:

1. Tap once on the **Audio & Visual** button in the Hearing section and drag this button **On** to enable **Mono Audio**

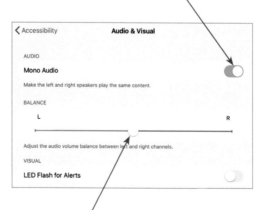

2. Drag this button to specify whether sound comes out of the left or right speaker

...cont'd

AssistiveTouch

This can be used by anyone who has difficulty navigating around the iPad with the screen or buttons. It can be used with an external device such as a joystick, or it can be used on its own. To use AssistiveTouch (under **Physical and Motor > Touch**):

1 Tap once on the **AssistiveTouch** option

Don't forget

The **AssistiveTouch** options make it easier for anyone with difficulties clicking the **Home** button, or using Multitasking Gestures.

2 Drag this button **On** to activate the **AssistiveTouch** function

3 The AssistiveTouch icon appears on the screen and can be dragged around

4 Tap once on the AssistiveTouch icon to view its options

Hot tip

The AssistiveTouch **Home** button option can be used if the physical **Home** button is ever damaged or does not work.

5 Tap once on the **Home** icon to return to the Home screen

61

...cont'd

Don't forget

Tap on the **More** button in the **Device** window to select options for creating more gestures, shaking the iPad, capturing a screenshot and accessing the App Switcher window.

6 Tap on the **Device** icon in Step 4 on the previous page

7 Tap once to activate the required function, including changing the screen rotation and adjusting the volume

Guided Access

The Guided Access option allows for certain functionality within an app to be disabled so that individual tasks can be focused on without any other distractions. To use this:

1 Under the **General** heading, tap once on the **Guided Access** option

2 Drag this button **On** to activate the Guided Access functionality

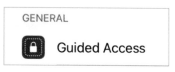

3 Open an app, and triple-click on the **Home** button to activate Guided Access within the app

4 Circle an area on the screen to disable it (this can be any functionality within the app). Tap on the **Start** button to activate Guided Access for that area. The circled area will not function within the app

3 iCloud

This chapter shows how to use the online iCloud services for storing and sharing content.

Living in the iCloud

iCloud is the Apple online service that performs a number of valuable functions:

- It makes your content available across multiple devices. The content is stored in the iCloud and then pushed out to other iCloud-enabled devices, including the iPhone, iPod Touch, and other Mac or Windows computers.

- It enables online access to your content via the iCloud website. This includes your iCloud email, Contacts, Calendar, Notes, and Reminders.

- It can back up the content of your iPad.

Once you have registered for and set up iCloud, it works automatically so you do not have to worry about anything. You can activate iCloud when you first set up your iPad, or:

Don't forget

It is free to register for and set up a standard iCloud account.

Hot tip

To access your iCloud account through the website, access **www.icloud.com** and enter your Apple ID details (see page 105).

1 Tap once on the **Settings** app

2 At the top of the Settings panel, tap once on the **Sign in to your iPad** option

3 If you already have an Apple ID, enter your details and tap once on the **Next** button

4 If you do not yet have an Apple ID, tap once on the **Don't have an Apple ID or forgot it?** link and follow the steps to create your Apple ID

...cont'd

iCloud settings

After you have set up your iCloud account you can then apply settings for how it works. Once you have done this, you will not have to worry about it again:

1. Tap once on the **Apple ID** tab of the Settings app

2. Tap once on the **iCloud** button

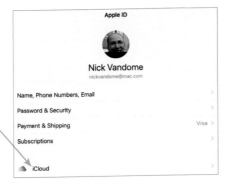

3. Drag these buttons **On** for items you want to be synced with iCloud. Each item is then saved and stored in the iCloud, and made available to other iCloud-enabled devices

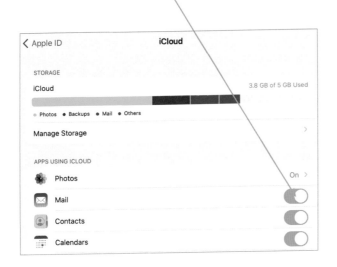

Tap once on the **Photos** option to access settings for storing and using your photos in iCloud.

Another useful iCloud function is the iCloud Keychain (**Settings > Apple ID > iCloud > Keychain**). If this is enabled, it can keep all of your passwords and credit card information up-to-date across multiple devices and remember them when you use them on websites. The information is encrypted and controlled through your Apple ID.

...cont'd

iCloud storage & backup

To view the storage on your iCloud account:

1 Tap once on the **Manage Storage** option in Step 3 on page 65

Manage Storage

2 The amount of storage that has been used is indicated by the colored bar at the top of the window (e.g. yellow for photos, purple for backups and blue for email)

< iCloud   **iCloud Storage**

iCloud   3.8 GB of 5 GB Used

● Photos ● Backups ● Mail ● Others

Change Storage Plan   5 GB >

3 Tap once on the **Change Storage Plan** button to increase the amount of storage (the default amount is 5GB, which is provided free of charge)

4 Select another storage plan as required, and tap once on the **Buy** button

Back   **Upgrade iCloud Storage**   Buy

iCloud stores the most important things from your device, like photos, documents, contacts, and more, so they're always available, even if you lose your device.

CURRENT PLAN

5GB   Free

CHOOSE UPGRADE

50GB   £0.79 per month   ✓

200GB   £2.49 per month
Can be shared with your family

2TB   £6.99 per month
Can be shared with your family

Don't forget

Prices are shown in local currencies.

About the iCloud Drive

One of the options in the iCloud section is for the iCloud Drive. This can be used to store documents so that you can use them on any other Apple devices that you have, such as an iPhone or a MacBook. With iCloud Drive (and the Files app) you can start work on a document on one device and continue on another device from where you left off.

1 Tap once on the **Apple ID** tab of the Settings app

2 Tap once on the **iCloud** button

3 By default, the iCloud Drive is set to **Off**

4 Slide the **iCloud Drive** button to green to turn it **On**

5 Drag the buttons **On** for the apps that you want to activate for syncing files with iCloud Drive. Content that you create with these apps will be stored in the iCloud Drive and be available within the same apps on other devices

If using iCloud Drive-compatible apps (such as **Pages**, **Numbers** and **Keynote**) they should be updated to their latest versions via the App Store.

Files App

Once the iCloud Drive has been activated within the iCloud settings, documents can be viewed and accessed using the Files app. This can be used to store documents and files that have been created on the iPad and also other online storage services, such as Dropbox and Google Drive. To start using the Files app:

Don't forget

By default, the Files app is on the Dock.

1 Tap once on the **Files** app

2 The Files app window shows items that are stored there, as specified by the selection in Step 5 on page 67

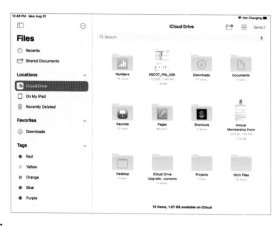

Hot tip

Tap once on the **Downloads** button in the left-hand sidebar to view items that have been downloaded from the web with Safari. See page 123 for details.

68

3 Tap once on the **iCloud Drive** button in Step 2 and tap once on a folder to view its contents. By default, the documents are stored in the iCloud. Tap once on an item to open it and download it to your iPad

Hot tip

Press and hold on a Files window and tap once on the **New Folder** button to add a new folder to the top level of the **Files** app, or within any of the existing folders.

...cont'd

4 Tap once on the **Select** button on the top toolbar

Select

5 Tap once on items to select them

6 Use the buttons on the bottom toolbar to **Share**, **Duplicate**, **Move**, or **Delete** the selected item(s)

| Share | Duplicate | Move | Delete |

7 If you have an account with online cloud-sharing services such as Dropbox or Google Drive, these will be available via the Files app, once you have downloaded the apps from the App Store and logged in to them

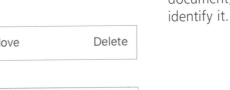

8 Tap the menu button at the top of the window once and tap on the **Edit Sidebar** button once to access buttons for turning the different services **On** or **Off**

Drag a file over one of the tags in the left-hand panel to add the tag to the document, to help identify it.

Tags	
●	Red
○	Yellow
●	Orange
●	Blue

Tap once on a location – i.e. Dropbox – to view its folder structure. Tap once on items within the folders to download them to your iPad.

...cont'd

Connecting a USB flashdrive

Some versions of the iPad Pro (2018 and later) have a USB-C Connector for charging the iPad, rather than the Lightning Connector. This also means that a USB flashdrive can be connected using the USB-C port on the iPad. The Files app can then be used to copy content from the flashdrive to the iPad. To do this:

1. Connect a USB flashdrive to the iPad. This can either be a USB-C flashdrive (with a USB-C Connector) or a USB-C adapter can be used for older USB flashdrives

2. Open the **Files** app. The flashdrive will show up under **Locations**

3. Tap once on the flashdrive to view its contents in the main Files window. Tap once on the **Select** button and tap once on the required items

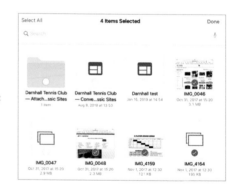

Select

4. Tap once on the **Move** button

5. Tap once on the **On My iPad** button and tap once on the **Copy** button to copy the items from the flashdrive to your iPad

Beware

Only some models of iPad support using USB flashdrives, even if they are running iPadOS 14. At the time of printing, the iPad Pro (2018 and later) and the iPad Air (4th generation) are the only models with a USB-C port for connecting flashdrives directly. A Lightning to USB adapter can be used to connect flashdrives to other models of iPad, but this does not mean they will support the use of the flashdrive.

About Family Sharing

In iPadOS 14, the Family Sharing function enables you to share items that you have downloaded from the App Store, such as music and movies, with up to six other family members, as long as they have an Apple ID Account. Once this has been set up, it is also possible to share items such as family calendars and photos, and even see where family members are on a map. To set up Family Sharing:

Hot tip

1. Access the **iCloud** section within the Settings app, as shown on page 65

If children are using Family Sharing you can specify that they have to ask permission before downloading content from the iTunes Store, the App Store or the Books Store. To do this, select them in the **Family Sharing** section of the **iCloud** settings and drag the **Ask To Buy** button **On**. For each purchase you will be sent a notification asking for approval.

2. Tap once on the **Family Sharing** button

3. Tap once on the **Set Up Your Family** button

4. Tap once on the **Invite People** button to invite family members, or friends, to join your Family Sharing. This includes music, storage plans, iTunes and App Store purchases, and location sharing for finding a lost or stolen Apple device

Invite People

5. Complete the setup process by confirming your iCloud account, and specify a payment method for items that are purchased through Family Sharing

Using Family Sharing

Once you have set up Family Sharing and added family members, you can start sharing a selection of items.

Sharing photos

Photos can be shared with Family Sharing thanks to the Family album that is created automatically within the Photos app. To use this:

1 Tap once on the **Photos** app

2 Tap once on this button to access the sidebar

3 The **Family** album is already available in the **Shared Albums** section. Tap once on the album to open it

4 Tap once on this button to add photos to the album

Family

+

5 Tap on the photos you want to add, and tap once on the **Done** button

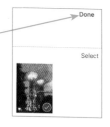

6 Make sure the **Family** album is selected as the Shared Album, and tap once on the **Post** button

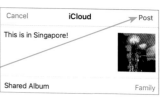

Beware

Shared Albums has to be turned **On** to enable sharing photos with other family members (**Settings > Photos > Shared Albums**).

Hot tip

When someone else in your Family Sharing circle adds a photo to the Family album, you are notified in the Notification Center and also by a red notification badge on the Photos app.

72

Sharing calendars

Family Sharing also generates a Family calendar that can be used by all Family Sharing members:

1 Tap once on the **Calendar** app

2 Create a calendar event (as shown on pages 138-139), tap on the **Calendar** button and select the Family calendar to add the event to a calendar that all members of Family Sharing can see

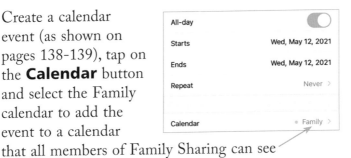

Hot tip

To change the color tag for a calendar, tap once on the **Calendars** button at the bottom-middle of the Calendar window. All of the current calendars will be shown. Tap once on the **i** symbol next to a calendar, and select a new color as required.

Sharing music, books and movies

Family Sharing means that all members of the group can share purchases from the iTunes Store, the App Store or the Books apps. To do this:

1 Open either the **iTunes Store**, **App Store** or **Books** apps

Hot tip

The Account icon in the App Store app and the Books app is the one containing the photo that you use for your Apple ID, located at the top of the window.

2 Access the **Purchased** section for the selected app. (For the **App Store**, tap once on the Account icon and tap once on the **Purchased** button; for the **iTunes Store**, tap once on the **Purchased** button on the bottom toolbar; for the **Books** app, tap once on the Account icon)

...cont'd

3 For all three apps, tap once on a member under the **Family Purchases** heading to view their purchases and download them, if required, by tapping once on this button

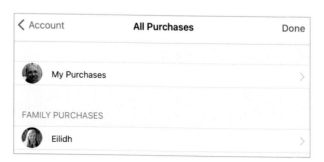

When the **Find My** app is opened, tap once on the **People** button to see people who have been added via Family Sharing. They must also have Location Services turned **On** (**Settings > Privacy > Location Services**) so that you can locate them. Tap once on the **Devices** button to view all of the Apple devices that can be located with the Find My app, including your own and those of any family members who have been added.

Finding family members

Family Sharing makes it easy to keep in touch with the rest of the family and see exactly where they are. This can be done with the Find My app. The other person must have their iPad (or other Apple device) turned on and be online. To find family members:

1 Tap once on the **Find My** app

2 The location of any people who are linked via your Family Sharing is displayed. Tap once on a person's name under 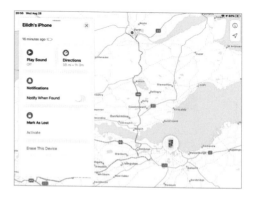 the **People** button (see tip) to view their location. Swipe outwards with thumb and forefinger to zoom in on the map and see the precise location

4 Keyboard and Apple Pencil

The iPad has a virtual keyboard and can also be used with an external one. This chapter shows how to manage the keyboard, and the Apple Pencil, for entering and editing text.

It's Virtually a Keyboard

The keyboard on the iPad is a virtual one; i.e. it appears on the touchscreen whenever text or numbered input is required for an app. This can be for a variety of reasons:

- Entering text with a word processing app, email, or an organization app such as Notes.

- Entering a web address into a web browser such as the Safari app.

- Entering information into a form.

- Entering a password.

Viewing the keyboard

When you attempt one of the items above, the keyboard appears so that you can enter any text or numbers:

Around the keyboard

To access the various keyboard controls:

In addition to the iPad virtual keyboard, it is also possible to use a traditional computer keyboard with the iPad. This is the Apple Smart Keyboard (see page 13). Other physical keyboards are also available for use with the iPad, including the Apple Wireless Keyboard, which connects via Bluetooth. This can be turned on in the Settings app, under the Bluetooth tab.

Don't forget

To return from Caps Lock, tap again on the **Shift/Caps** button.

1 Tap once on the **Shift** button to create a **Cap** (capital) text letter

2 Double-tap on the **Shift** button to enable **Caps Lock**

3 Tap once on this button to back-delete an item

Additional buttons

In iPadOS 14, letters, numbers and symbols can all be accessed from a single keyboard. To do this:

Swipe down on one of the keys on the top line of the keyboard to enter the equivalent number, rather than a letter

If a key has a symbol above the letter, swipe down on it to enter the symbol

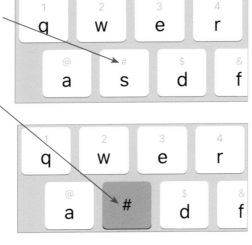

Tap once on this button to hide the keyboard

Hot tip

If you are entering a password, or details into a form, the virtual keyboard will have a **Go** or **Send** button that can be used to activate the information that has been entered.

Don't forget

The virtual keyboard changes slightly according to the app you are using. For instance, in the Mail app the keyboard differs depending on whether you are adding a recipient (the @ key appears on the keyboard) or adding body text.

@

Moving the Keyboard

By default, the keyboard appears as a single unit along the bottom of the screen. However, it is possible to undock the keyboard and also split it to appear on either side of the screen. To do this:

Hot tip

To redock the keyboard, press and hold on the button in Step 1 and tap once on the **Dock** button or, if the keyboard has been split, the **Dock and Merge** button.

Hot tip

The keyboard can also be split by swiping outwards on both sides, with one finger on each side. Reverse the process to merge it again.

1 Press and hold this button on the keyboard

2 Tap once on the **Undock** button

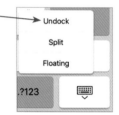

3 The keyboard is undocked from the bottom of the screen

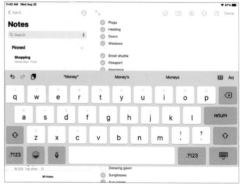

4 Tap once on the **Split** button in Step 2

5 The keyboard is split to the left and the right sides of the screen

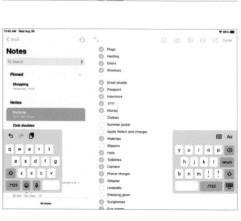

Floating keyboard

In addition to the iPad keyboard being undocked and split, it can also be used at any point on the screen, so that you can position it wherever you want. This is known as the floating keyboard. To use it:

1 Press and hold this button on the keyboard

2 Tap once on the **Floating** button

3 The keyboard is reduced to its own panel within the current window

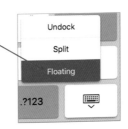

4 Press on the bar at the bottom of the keyboard and drag it to move it around the screen

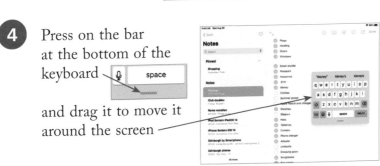

Hot tip

Floating mode for the keyboard can also be activated by pinching inwards on the keyboard with two fingers. Swipe outwards with two fingers to return it to its default state.

Hot tip

The floating keyboard can also be returned to its default state by dragging it to the bottom of the window.

Entering Text

Once you have applied the keyboard settings that you require, you can start entering text. To do this:

1 Tap once on the text entry area to activate the keyboard. Start typing with the keyboard. The text will appear at the point where you tapped on the screen

If Predictive text is **On**, the suggested word will appear above the keyboard on the QuickType bar (see page 84).

2 If Predictive text is **Off**, as you type, Auto-Correction comes up with suggestions. Tap once on the spacebar to accept the suggestion, or tap once on the cross next to it to reject it

3 Any misspelled words appear underlined in red

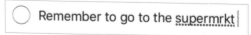

If you keep typing as normal, the Auto-Correction suggestion will disappear when you finish the word.

4 Tap once on this button to hide the keyboard

Editing Text

Once text has been entered it can be selected, copied, cut and pasted. Depending on the app being used, the text can also be formatted, such as with a word processing app.

Managing text
To work with text in a document you have created:

1 To change the insertion point in a document, press on the cursor to pick it up

2 Drag the cursor to move the insertion point

3 Tap once at the insertion point to access the menu buttons

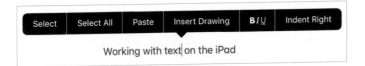

4 Double-tap on a word to select it. Tap once on one of the menu buttons, as required

5 Use the Shortcuts bar on the keyboard to, from left to right: cut the selection; copy the selection; or paste an item

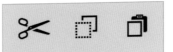

Hot tip

Once the menu buttons in Step 3 have been accessed, tap once on **Select** to select the previous word, or **Select All** to select all of the available text.

81

Hot tip

The menu buttons in Step 4 can be used to replace the selected word; add bold, italics or underlining to it; or view a definition of it (Look Up).

...cont'd

Selecting text

Text can be selected using a range of methods:

Don't forget

Once text has been selected, there are a range of gestures that can be used to copy and paste it, and also undo the previous action. To copy selected text: pinch inwards over the text with thumb and two fingers. To paste text: swipe outwards with thumb and two fingers, in a dropping motion. To undo the previous action: swipe from right to left with three fingers.

1 Double-tap on a word to select it

> Moving the cursor using iPadOS.

2 Drag the selection handles to increase or decrease the selection. This is a good way to select certain text within a sentence or within a paragraph

> Moving the cursor using iPadOS.

3 Triple-tap on a word to select the whole of its related sentence

> The onscreen keyboard is always there for responding to email or taking notes. You can also use a physical keyboard like the Smart Keyboard if you want one. And with iPadOS, there are more ways to use both however you want.

4 Quadruple-tap on a word to select the whole of its related paragraph

> The onscreen keyboard is always there for responding to email or taking notes. You can also use a physical keyboard like the Smart Keyboard if you want one. And with iPadOS, there are more ways to use both however you want.

Keyboard Settings

Settings for the keyboard can be determined in the **General** section of the Settings app. To do this:

1 Select **Settings** > **General** and tap once on the **Keyboard** option

Keyboard

2 Drag the **Auto-Capitalization** button **On** to ensure letters will automatically be capitalized at the beginning of a sentence

3 Drag the **Auto-Correction** button **On** to ensure suggestions for words will appear as you type

4 Drag the **Check Spelling** button **On** to spell-check words as you type

5 Drag the **Enable Caps Lock** button **On** to enable this function to be performed

6 Drag the **"."** **Shortcut** button (further down the Keyboard settings screen) **On** to enable the functionality for adding a period/full stop with a double-tap of the spacebar

7 Tap once on the **Keyboards** option to access options for adding different keyboards

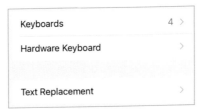

8 Tap once on the **Text Replacement** option to view existing text shortcuts and also to create new ones

The **Auto-Correction** function works as you type a word, so it may change a number of times, depending on the length of the word you are typing.

For more information about Text Replacement, see page 87.

Using Predictive Text

Predictive text tries to guess what you are typing, and also predicts the next word following the one you have just typed. It was developed primarily for text messaging, and it is included on the iPad with iPadOS 14. To use it:

Don't forget

Predictive text learns from your writing style as you write, and so gets more accurate at predicting words.

Hot tip

Third-party virtual keyboards can be downloaded from the App Store and added to your iPad. Search "keyboard" in the App Store Search box. Keyboards that have been added (and also those for different languages) can be activated within **Settings** > **General** > **Keyboard** > **Keyboards** > **Add New Keyboard**. Press and hold on this button on the keyboard to switch between available keyboards.

1 Tap once on the **General** tab in the Settings app

2 Tap once on the **Keyboard** option

Keyboard

3 Drag the **Predictive** button **On**

4 When Predictive text is activated, the QuickType bar is displayed above the keyboard. Initially, this has a suggestion for the first word to include. Tap on a word, or start typing

5 As you type, suggestions appear. Tap on one to accept it. Tap on the word within the quotation marks to accept exactly what you have typed, or tap on another option

6 After you have typed a word, a suggestion for the next word appears. This can be selected by tapping on it, or ignored

84

Slide Typing

When using a floating keyboard on the iPad (see page 79) it is possible to type words by sliding your fingers across the keyboard between letters, rather than having to tap on each one individually. This is also known as QuickPath typing and it is a useful way to type with one hand with the floating keyboard. To use slide typing:

1 Tap once on the **General** tab in the Settings app

2 Tap once on the **Keyboard** option

Keyboard

3 Drag the **Slide on Floating Keyboard to Type** button **On**

Slide on Floating Keyboard to Type	⬤

4 Activate the floating keyboard as shown on page 79. Words can be created by sliding your finger across the relevant letters on the keyboard. A light trail is produced as you slide over the keyboard. If Predictive text is being used, suggested words appear on the QuickType bar as you slide over the keyboard. Release your finger to use the suggested word

Beware

Slide typing can take a bit of getting used to, but once it has been mastered it is an efficient way to create short pieces of text: longer blocks of text are best done with the keyboard in the normal way.

Keyboard Shortcuts

There are two types of shortcuts that can be used on the iPad keyboard:

- Shortcuts using keys on the keyboard

- Shortcuts created with text abbreviations

Shortcuts with keys
The shortcuts that can be created with the keys on the keyboard are:

Hot tip

The shortcut in Step 1 can be disabled by switching off the **"."** **Shortcut** option within the **Settings** > **General** > **Keyboard** section.

1 Double-tap on the spacebar to add a full stop/period and a space at the end of a sentence

2 Swipe up once on the comma (or press and hold) to insert an apostrophe

3 Swipe up once on the full stop/period to insert quotation marks

4 Press and hold on appropriate letters to access accented versions for different languages

Text abbreviations

To create shortcuts with text abbreviations:

1 Tap once on the **Keyboard** option in the **General** section of the Settings app

Keyboard

Don't forget

The shortcut does not need to have the equivalent number of letters as words in the phrase. A 10-word phrase could have a two-letter shortcut.

2 Tap once on the **Text Replacement** option

Text Replacement

3 Tap once on this button to add a new shortcut +

4 Enter the phrase you want to be made into a shortcut

Phrase   My name is Nick

5 Enter the abbreviation you want to use as the shortcut for the phrase

Shortcut   mnn

Hot tip

To use a shortcut, enter the abbreviation. As you type, the phrase appears underneath the abbreviation. Tap once on the spacebar to add the phrase, or tap once on the cross to reject it. To delete a shortcut, in the **Text Replacement** section in Step 7 swipe on it from right to left and tap once on the **Delete** button.

6 Tap once on the **Save** button

Save

7 The shortcut is displayed here

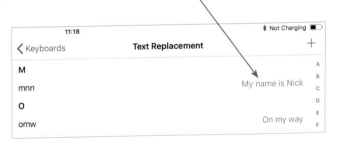

8 Use the Search box or the alphabetical bar at the right-hand side to search for other shortcuts that have been created

87

Using the Apple Pencil

The Apple Pencil is an excellent option for getting creative with drawing apps and it is also very effective in a range of text tasks, including converting handwriting, deleting text and selecting text.

Scribble

The Apple Pencil can be used to create handwritten text in compatible apps. In some cases this can then be converted automatically into typed text. This works in any text field and the text can then be edited in several ways. This is known as Scribble. To use Scribble with the Apple Pencil:

The Scribble options with the Apple Pencil are a new feature in iPadOS 14.

The Scribble option is activated in **Settings** > **Apple Pencil** and by dragging the **Scribble** button **On**.

1 In a text box, or a search box, use the Apple Pencil to enter handwritten text

2 When you finish writing a word, it will be converted to typed text, with relevant options displayed, depending on the text box in which it is entered

The Apple Pencil can also be used to create handwritten text in the Notes app, which can also be converted to typed text. See pages 134-135 for details.

Deleting text

Text in a text field (including a web browser address bar) can be deleted using the Apple Pencil. This can be done if it is entered as handwriting and then converted to text, or entered directly from the keyboard:

The options for deleting and selecting text with the Apple Pencil are new features in iPadOS 14.

1 Enter text into a text box or web browser

Q in easy sters

2 If there is a mistake in a word, scribble over it with the Apple Pencil

Q in easy ~~sters~~

3 The word is deleted

Q in easy

Selecting text

The Apple Pencil can also be used to select text in a text field, after which editing options can be applied to it.

Hot tip

Press and hold with the Apple Pencil in any text field, to create a space to write or type another word.

1 Circle the required text item with the Apple Pencil. This can be a single word, or several

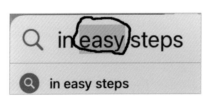

Q in easy steps

2 The circled text is selected and available editing options are displayed

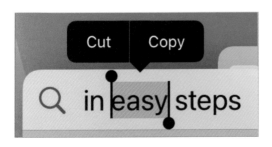

Hot tip

Draw a line between letters to create a space between them, or draw a line in the space between two words to remove the space and join the words together.

Voice Typing

On the keyboard there is also a voice-typing option, which enables you to enter text by speaking into a microphone, rather than typing on the keyboard. This is On by default.

Using voice typing

Voice typing can be used with any app with a text input function. To do this:

Beware

Voice typing is not an exact science, and you may find that some strange examples appear. The best results are created if you speak as clearly as possible and reasonably slowly.

Hot tip

The first time that you tap on the **Microphone** button you may be prompted to select the **Enable Dictation** button too. This can also be done within **Settings** > **General** > **Keyboard** > **Enable Dictation**.

Don't forget

There are other voice-typing apps available from the App Store. Two to try are Dragon Anywhere and Voice Dictation, Voice to Text.

1 Tap once on this button on the keyboard to activate the voice-typing microphone. Speak into the microphone to record text

2 As the voice-typing function is processing the recording, this screen appears

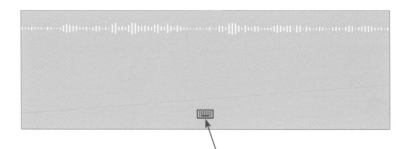

3 Tap once on the **Keyboard** button to finish recording and return to the virtual keyboard

4 Once the recording has been processed, the text appears in the app

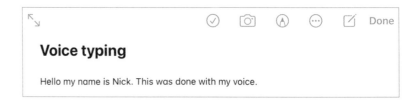

Voice typing

Hello my name is Nick. This was done with my voice.

5 Knowing your Apps

Apps keep the iPad engine running. This chapter details the built-in ones and shows how to review and download more through the App Store.

You need an active internet connection to download apps from the App Store.

Within a number of apps there is a **Share** button that can be used to share items through a variety of methods, including email, Messages, Facebook and Twitter. The Share button can also be used to share items using the AirDrop function over short distances with other compatible Apple devices (see page 30). To access these options, tap once on this button, where available.

What is an App?

An app is just a more modern name for a computer program. Initially, it was used in relation to mobile devices, such as the iPhone and the iPad, but it is now becoming more widely used with desktop and laptop computers, for both Mac and Windows operating systems.

On the iPad there are two types of apps:

● **Built-in apps**. These are the apps that come pre-installed on the iPad.

● **App Store apps**. These are apps that can be downloaded from the online App Store. There is a huge range of apps available there, covering a variety of different categories. Some are free, while others have to be paid for. The apps in the App Store are updated and added to on a daily basis, so there are always new ones to explore.

There are also two important points to remember about apps (both built-in and those from the App Store):

● Apart from some of the built-in apps, the majority of apps do not interact with each other. This means that there is less chance of viruses being transmitted from app to app on your iPad, and apps can also operate without a reliance on other apps.

● Content created by apps is saved within the app itself, rather than within a file structure on your iPad – e.g. if you create a note in the Notes app, it is saved there; if you take a photo, it is saved in the Photos app. Content is also usually saved automatically when it is created or edited, so you do not have to worry about saving as you work.

Built-in Apps

The built-in iPad apps are the ones that appear on the Home screen when you turn on the iPad:

Some of the built-in apps appear on the second Home screen of the iPad.

The iPad **Settings** app is another of the built-in apps, and this is looked at in detail on pages 24-25.

- **App Store**. This can be used to access the App Store, from where additional apps can then be downloaded.

- **Books**. This is an app for downloading electronic books, which can then be read on the iPad. This can be done for both plain text and illustrated items.

- **Calendar**. An app for storing appointments, important dates and other calendar information. It can be synced with iCloud.

You need an Apple ID to obtain content from the **Books** app. Books are downloaded in a matter of seconds, and you cannot change your mind once you have entered your Apple ID details. For full details about obtaining an Apple ID, see page 105.

- **Camera**. This gives direct access to the front-facing and rear-facing iPad cameras. You can also access your Photos gallery from here.

- **Clock**. This displays the current time and can be used to view the time in different countries, and also as an alarm clock and a stopwatch.

- **Contacts**. An address book app. Once contacts are added here they can then also be accessed from other apps, such as Mail.

...cont'd

● **FaceTime**. This is an app that uses the built-in front-facing camera on the iPad to hold video chats with other iPad users, or those with an iPhone, iPod Touch or a Mac computer.

● **Files**. This app can be used to display and access files held on your iPad, in the iCloud Drive, and other online file storage services such as Dropbox.

● **Find My**. This is an app that can be used to view the location of anyone who is part of your Family Sharing group in iCloud and also locate any other linked Apple devices.

● **Home**. This can be used to control certain compatible functions within the home, such as heating controls.

There have to be compatible devices in the home in order for the **Home** app to work with them. Check out Smart Homes in easy steps at www.ineasysteps.com for more help with this.

● **iTunes Store**. This app can be used to browse the iTunes store, where music, TV shows, movies, and more can be downloaded to your iPad.

● **Mail**. This is the email app for sending and receiving email on your iPad.

● **Maps**. Use this app to view maps from around the world, find specific locations, and get directions to destinations.

● **Measure**. This can be used to measure objects, using the iPad's camera.

Don't forget

Some of the built-in apps, such as **Mail** and **Contacts**, interact with each other when required. However, since these are designed by Apple, there is little chance of them containing viruses.

● **Messages**. This is the iPad messaging service, which can be used between iPads, iPhones, iPod Touches and Mac computers. It can be used with not only text, but also photos and videos.

● **Music**. An app for playing music on your iPad and also accessing the Apple Music service, which connects to the whole iTunes library.

- **News**. This is an app that collates news stories and content from numerous sources.

- **Notes**. If you need to jot down your thoughts or ideas, this app is perfect for just that.

- **Photo Booth**. This is an app for creating fun and creative effects with your photos.

- **Photos**. This is an app for viewing and editing photos, creating slideshows, and for viewing the videos you have taken with your iPad camera. It can also be used to share photos via iCloud.

It is worth investing in a good pair of headphones for listening to music and podcasts, so you do not disturb other people.

- **Podcasts**. This can be used to download and play podcasts from within the App Store.

- **Reminders**. Use this app for organization, when you want to create to-do lists and set reminders for events.

- **Safari**. The Apple web browser that has been developed for viewing the web on your iPad.

- **Stocks**. This can be used to display real-time stock prices and related news from Apple News.

- **Tips**. This can be used to display tips and hints for items on your iPad.

- **TV**. Previously called the Video app, this is an app for viewing videos purchased from the Apple TV Store on your iPad, and also streaming them to a larger HDTV monitor.

- **Voice Memos**. This can be used to record and share voice recordings.

About the App Store

While the built-in apps that come with the iPad are flexible and versatile, it really comes into its own when you connect to the App Store. This is an online resource containing thousands of apps that can be downloaded and then used on your iPad, including categories from Lifestyle to Travel.

To use the App Store, you must first have an Apple ID. This can be obtained when you first connect to the App Store. Once you have an Apple ID, you can start exploring the App Store:

Don't forget

For full details about obtaining an Apple ID, see page 105.

Don't forget

Tap once on the **Get** button to download a free app (a paid-for one will display a price).

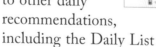

Don't forget

The **Arcade** section is a monthly subscription service that contains an extensive range of games.

1. Tap once on the **App Store** app on the Home screen

2. The App Store Home screen (**Today**) displays the latest current recommended apps, on a daily basis. Swipe up the page to move to other daily recommendations, including the Daily List

3. Tap on the buttons on the bottom toolbar to view the apps according to **Today**, **Games**, **Apps**, and **Arcade**

4. Tap once on an app to view its details

5. Swipe up the page to view more information about the app

Finding Apps

Within the App Store, apps are separated into categories according to type. To find apps in the App Store:

1 Tap once on the **Apps** button on the bottom toolbar

2 Details of the latest apps are displayed

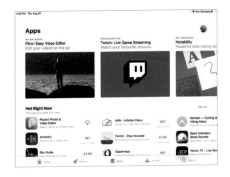

Don't forget

Some apps will differ depending on the geographical location from where you are accessing the App Store.

3 Scroll down the page (by swiping up) to view the different sections. Tap once on the **See All** button to view all of the items in a section

Hot tip

You can buy bundles of apps from some developers at a reduced price.

Categories

To view the different categories in the App Store:

1 Tap once on the **Apps** button on the bottom toolbar

2 Swipe up the page to the **Top Categories** section

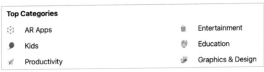

3 Tap once on the **See All** button to view all of the available categories. Tap once on a category to view the apps within it

Don't forget

When viewing apps within a specific category, swipe up the page to view the **Top Paid** and **Top Free** apps for the category.

Don't forget

Another way to find apps is with the App Store Search button, which is located at the right of the bottom toolbar of the App Store. To use this: tap once on the Search button and tap

once in the Search box to bring up the iPad virtual keyboard. Enter a search keyword or phrase. Suggestions appear as you are typing. Tap once on a result to view the related app and information about it.

Beware

Do not limit yourself to just viewing the top apps. Although these are the most popular, there are also a lot of excellent apps within each category.

...cont'd

Top Charts
To find the top-rated apps:

1 Tap once on the **Apps** button on the bottom toolbar

2 Swipe up the page to view the current **Top Paid Apps** and **Top Free Apps**

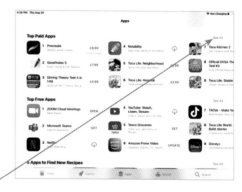

3 Tap once on the **See All** button to see the full range of paid-for and free apps

See All

4 Tap once on the **All Apps** button, and tap once on a category to view the Top Paid and Top Free apps for that category

All Apps

Obtaining Apps

When you identify an app that you would like to use, it can be downloaded to your iPad. To do this:

1 Find the app you want to download, and tap once on the button next to the app (this will say **Get** or will have a price)

2 Tap once on the **Install** button

3 The app will begin to download onto your iPad, indicated by this icon next to it in the App Store

4 Once the app is downloaded it will appear in the next available space on one of the Home screens. Tap once on the app to open and use it

Apps usually download in a few minutes or less, depending on the speed of your internet connection.

Some apps have "in-app purchases". This is additional content that has to be paid for when it is downloaded.

Updating Apps

The world of apps is a dynamic and fast-moving one, and new apps are being created and added to the App Store on a daily basis. Existing apps are also being updated, to improve their performance, security and functionality. Once you have installed an app from the App Store, it is possible to obtain updates at no extra cost (whether or not the app was paid for). To do this:

Hot tip

You should keep your apps as up-to-date as possible to take advantage of software fixes and updates.

Hot tip

If updates are not set to be downloaded automatically, a notification badge will appear on the App Store icon to indicate that updates are available. These can then be updated in the **Account** section of the App Store, under the **Available Updates** heading.

Hot tip

The notification badge on apps (such as the **App Store** and the **Mail** app) can be turned On or Off in **Settings > Notifications > [select app]** > drag the **Badges** button **On** or **Off**.

1 Set updates to be downloaded automatically: **Settings > App Store >** and drag **App Updates On**

App Updates

2 Tap once on the **App Store** app

3 In the App Store, tap once on the **Account** button, located at the top right-hand side of the screen

4 The available updates are displayed under the **Upcoming Automatic Updates** heading. If automatic updates have been selected in Step 1, the available

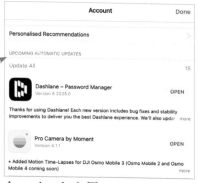

updates will have been downloaded. Tap once on the **Open** button to open the latest version

5 If automatic updates have not been selected, each item will have an **Update** button next to it, and there will also be an **Update All** button

Organizing Apps

When you start downloading apps you will probably soon find that you have dozens, if not hundreds, of them. You can move between screens to view all of your apps by swiping left or right with one finger. It is also possible to organize apps into individual folders to make using them more manageable. To do this:

Hot tip

To move an app between screens, press and hold on it until it starts to jiggle and a cross appears in the corner. Then, drag it to the side of the screen. If there is space on the next screen, the app will be moved to the point at which it is released.

1 Press on an app until it starts to jiggle and a cross appears at the top-left corner

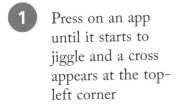

2 Drag the app over another one

Beware

Only top-level folders can be created; i.e. sub-folders cannot be created. Also, one folder cannot be placed within another.

3 A folder is created, containing the two apps. The folder is given a default name, usually based on the category of the apps

4 Tap on the folder name, and type a new name if required

Hot tip

If you want to rename an apps folder after it has been created, press and hold on it until it starts to jiggle. Then tap on it once and edit the name, as in Step 4.

5 Click the **Home** button once to finish creating the folder, and click it again to return to the Home screen. The folder is added on the Home screen. Tap once on this to access the items within it

Deleting Apps

If you decide that you do not want certain apps anymore, they can be deleted from your iPad. However, they remain in the iCloud so that you can reinstall them if you change your mind. This also means that if you delete an app by mistake, you can get it back from the App Store without having to pay for it again. To delete an app:

If you delete an app it will also delete any data that has been compiled with that app, even if you reinstall it from the App Store.

1 Press on an app until it starts to jiggle and a cross appears at the top-left corner

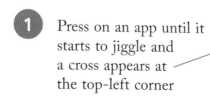

iTunes U

2 Tap once on the cross to delete the app. In the Delete dialog box, tap once on the **Delete** button. The app is then uninstalled from your iPad

Delete "iTunes U"?
Deleting this app will also delete its data.

Cancel   Delete

To reinstall an app:

Don't forget

In iPadOS 14 some, but not all, of the built-in apps can be deleted. This is done in the same way as for deleting an app, shown on this page.

1 Tap once on the **App Store** app

App Store

2 Tap once on the **Search** button on the bottom toolbar

🔍 Search

3 Enter the name of the app in the Search box, and tap once on the **iCloud** icon to download it again

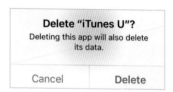

Filters ⌄   🔍 itunes u

iTunes U
Free educational courses
★★★★☆ 12   ☁️

6 Keeping in Touch

This chapter shows how to use your iPad to keep ahead in the fast-moving world of online communications, using email, social media, video calls, and a range of texting options.

Getting Online

iPads can be used for a variety of different communications, but they all require online access. This is done via Wi-Fi, and you will need to have an Internet Service Provider and a Wi-Fi router to connect to the internet. Once this is in place, you will be able to connect to a Wi-Fi network.

Don't forget

If you have the 4G/3G version of the iPad you can obtain internet access this way, but this has to be done through a provider of this service, as with a cell/mobile phone.

1 Tap once on the **Settings** app

2 Tap once on the **Wi-Fi** tab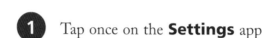

3 Ensure the **Wi-Fi** button is in the **On** position

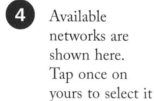

4 Available networks are shown here. Tap once on yours to select it

Don't forget

If you are connecting to your home Wi-Fi network, the iPad should connect automatically each time, once it has been set up. If you are connecting in a public Wi-Fi area, you will be asked which network you would like to join.

5 Enter the password for your Wi-Fi router

6 Tap once on the **Join** button Join

7 Once a network has been joined, a tick appears next to it. This now provides access to the internet

Obtaining an Apple ID

An Apple ID is an email address and password registered with Apple that enables you to log in and use a variety of online Apple services. These include:

- App Store

- iTunes Store and Apple Music

- iCloud

- Messages

- FaceTime

- Books

It is free to register for an Apple ID, and this can be done when you access one of the apps or services that require it, or you can register on the Apple website at Apple ID (**https://appleid.apple.com**):

If you are using an Apple ID to buy items such as from iTunes or the App Store, you will need to provide a valid method of payment.

105

1   Tap once on the **Create Your Apple ID** button at the top of the Apple ID web page

Create your Apple ID >

2   Enter the details for the **Create Your Apple ID** wizard to set up your Apple ID Account

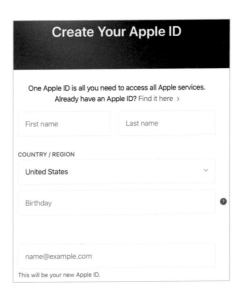

Create Your Apple ID

One Apple ID is all you need to access all Apple services.
Already have an Apple ID? Find it here >

First name | Last name

COUNTRY / REGION

United States

Birthday

name@example.com

This will be your new Apple ID.

Settings > **Apple ID** is where you can access your Apple ID details and edit them, if required.

Setting up an Email Account

Email accounts

Email settings can be specified within the Settings app. Different email accounts can also be added. To do this:

Hot tip

If you don't already have an email account set up, you can choose one of the providers from the list and you will be guided through the setup process.

Hot tip

If your email provider is not on the **Add Account** list, tap once on **Other** at the bottom of the list and complete the account details using the information from your email provider.

1 Tap once on the **Settings** app

2 Tap once on the **Mail** tab

3 Tap once on the **Add Account** option to add a new account

4 Tap once on the type of email account you want to add

5 Enter your login details for the account. Follow the wizard for the account, and tap on the **Next** button at each stage

6 Drag these buttons **On** or **Off** to specify which functions are to be available for the required account

7 Each new account is added under the **Accounts** heading of the Accounts section

Email settings

Email settings can be specified within the Settings app. Different email accounts can also be added there.

1 Under the **Mail** section, there are several options for how Mail operates and looks. These include the number of lines for previewing an email in the Inbox, options for managing emails by swiping on them, and options for blocking emails

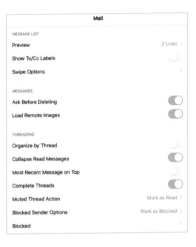

If you set up more than one email account, messages from all of them can be downloaded and displayed by **Mail**.

The **Organize by Thread** option can be turned **On** to show connected email conversations within your Inbox. If there is a thread of emails, this is indicated by this symbol:

Tap on it once to view the thread.

Emailing

Email on the iPad is created, sent and received using the Mail app. This provides a range of options for managing email, including adding mailboxes and viewing email conversation threads.

Accessing Mail

To access Mail, and start sending and receiving emails:

Hot tip

To quickly delete an email from your Inbox, swipe on it from right to left and tap once on the **Trash** (Delete) button. This also generates an option to **Flag** the email, and a **More** button from which you can reply, forward, mark or move the current email.

1 Tap once on the **Mail** app (the red icon in the corner displays the number of unread emails in your Inbox)

2 Tap once on a message to display it in the main panel

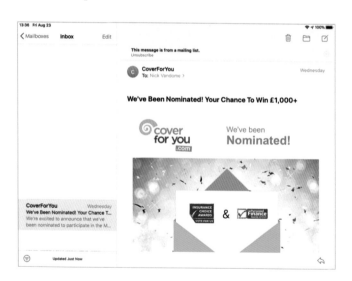

Don't forget

If the **Fetch New Data** option (**Settings** > **Mail** > **Accounts** > **Fetch New Data**) is set to **Push**, new emails will be downloaded automatically from your mail server.
To check manually for new downloads, swipe down from the top of the mailbox pane.

3 Use these buttons to, from left to right: delete the current message, move it to another folder or create a new message (see next page)

4 Tap once on this button, at the bottom-right of the Mail window to reply to a message, forward it to a new recipient, delete it, move it to another folder, or mark it as read or unread

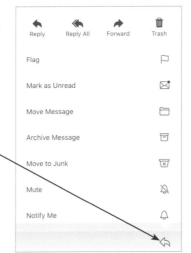

Reply	Reply All	Forward	Trash
Flag	
Mark as Unread	
Move Message	
Archive Message	
Move to Junk	
Mute	
Notify Me	

Creating email
To create and send an email:

1 Tap once on this button to create a new message

2 In the **To:** box, enter the recipient's email address, or type the recipient's name (if they are in your **Contacts** app), and tap on one of the suggestions to select it

Cancel

New Message

To: ei

c.com

To

Eilidh
eilidhvandome@googlemail.com

3 Enter a subject

Enter the body text

Cancel

Lunch tomorrow

To: Eilidh

Cc/Bcc, From: nickvandome@mac.com

Subject: Lunch tomorrow

Hi, where would you like to go for lunch?

Tap once on the **Send** button to send the email to the recipient

Hot tip

If the recipient has been added to your **Contacts** app (see page 140), their details will appear as you type. Tap once on the email address, if it appears, to include it in the **To:** box.

...cont'd

Mailboxes

Different categories of email messages can be managed via Mailboxes. For instance, you may want to keep your social emails separate from ones that apply to financial activities.

Hot tip

Messages can be edited within individual mailboxes. To do this, select a mailbox and tap once on the **Edit** button. The message can then be edited with the **Mark**, **Move** or **Trash/Delete** options at the bottom of the window.

Don't forget

One mailbox that can be included is for VIPs; i.e. your most important contacts. To add these from an email, tap and hold on the person's name in an email you receive from them, then tap once on the **Add to VIP** button. Under **Mailboxes**, tap once on **VIP** to view emails from all of your VIPs.

1 From your Inbox, tap once on the **Mailboxes** button

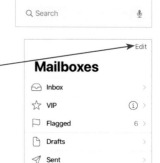

2 The current mailboxes are displayed. Tap once on the **Edit** button

3 Tap once on the **New Mailbox** button at the bottom of the Mailboxes panel

New Mailbox

4 Enter a name for the new mailbox. Tap once on the **Save** button

5 Tap once on the **Done** button

Done

6 To delete a mailbox, tap on it from the Edit window accessed in Step 2. In the subsequent **Edit Mailbox** window, tap on the **Delete Mailbox** button

Adding Social Media

Using social media sites such as Facebook, Instagram and Twitter to keep in touch with family and friends has now become common across all generations. On the iPad with iPadOS 14, it is possible to download a range of social media apps and also view updates through the Notification Center (see second Hot tip). To add social media apps:

1. Open the App Store and navigate to the **Apps > Categories > Social Networking** section

 Social Networking

2. Tap once on the required apps to download them to your iPad

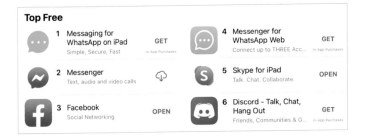

Top Free

1	Messaging for WhatsApp on iPad	Simple, Secure, Fast	GET In-App Purchases		
2	Messenger	Text, audio and video calls			
3	Facebook	Social Networking	OPEN		
4	Messenger for WhatsApp Web	Connect up to THREE Acc...	GET In-App Purchases		
5	Skype for iPad	Talk. Chat. Collaborate.	OPEN		
6	Discord - Talk, Chat, Hang Out	Friends, Communities & G...	GET In-App Purchases		

3. Tap once on an app to open it

Facebook

4. If you already have an account with the social media service, enter your login details, or tap once on the **Sign Up** button to create a new account

Phone number or email

Password

Log In

Sign Up for Facebook   Need Help?

Don't forget

Social media websites can also be accessed directly through the Safari web browser.

Hot tip

See page 118 for more about social networking apps.

Hot tip

Social media updates for some apps can be set to appear in your **Notification Center**. Open **Settings** and tap once on the **Notifications** tab. Under the **Notification Style** heading, tap once on the social networking site and select options for how you would like the notifications to appear.

112

You need an Apple ID to send iMessages and have to sign in with it when you start using the Messages app.

iMessages are sent using Wi-Fi. If a Wi-Fi connection is not available, the message cannot be sent, unless the iPad has a cellular network connection.

If an iPad has a cellular network connection then this can be used to send regular text messages to other compatible devices such as cell/mobile phones. If the recipient is not using iMessages, the message will be sent as a standard SMS (Short Message Service). By default, iMessages appear in blue bubbles and SMS messages in green bubbles.

Text Messaging

Text messaging should not be thought of as the domain of the younger generation. On your iPad you can join the world of text with the Apple iMessage service that is accessed via the Messages app. This enables text, photo, video, emojis and audio messages to be sent, free of charge, between users of iPadOS on the iPad, iOS on the iPhone and iPod Touch, and Mac computers. iMessages can be sent to cell/mobile phone numbers and email addresses.

1 Tap once on the **Messages** app

2 Tap once on this button to create a new message and start a new conversation

3 Tap once on this button to select someone from your contacts

4 Tap once on a contact to select them as the recipient of the new message

5 Tap once in the text box, and type with the keyboard to create a message. Tap once on this button to send the message

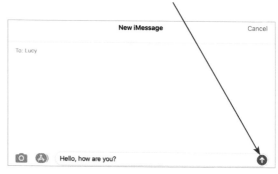

As the conversation progresses, each message is displayed in the main window

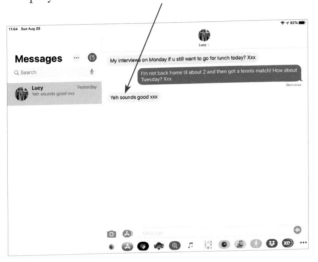

Hot tip

Press and hold on a message, and tap on the **More...** button that appears. Select a message, or messages, and tap on the **Trash** icon to remove them.

To edit whole conversations, tap once on the **Edit** button in the Messages panel and tap once on **Manage Messages List**

Manage Messages List

Edit Name and Photo

Don't forget

When a message has been sent, you are notified underneath it when it has been delivered.

8 Tap once here to select the conversation, and tap once on the **Delete** button at the bottom of the page to delete the conversation

Messages

Q Search

Lucy   Yesterday
Yeh sounds good xxx

Delete

Press and hold on a name in the Messages panel and tap once on the **Pin** button to pin this conversation at the top of the panel. This is a new feature in iPadOS 14.

Pin

Enhancing Text Messages

Adding emojis

Emojis (small graphical symbols) are becoming more common in text messages, and there is a huge range that can be included with iPadOS 14. To use these:

1 Tap once on this button on the keyboard to view the emoji keyboards

2 Swipe left and right to view the emoji options. Tap once on an emoji to add it to a message

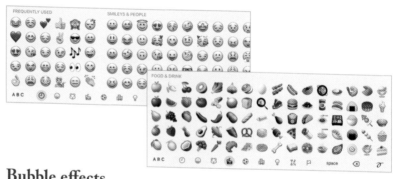

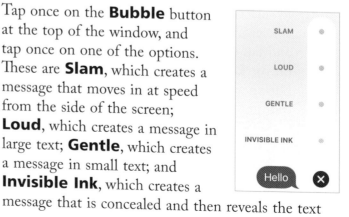

Bubble effects

iMessages can also be sent with certain animated effects:

1 Write a message and press and hold on this button

2 Tap once on the **Bubble** button at the top of the window, and tap once on one of the options. These are **Slam**, which creates a message that moves in at speed from the side of the screen; **Loud**, which creates a message in large text; **Gentle**, which creates a message in small text; and **Invisible Ink**, which creates a message that is concealed and then reveals the text

Screen effects

iMessages can also be sent with full-screen effects:

1 Repeat Step 1 for Bubble effects on the previous page and tap once on the **Screen** button at the top of the window. Swipe left and right to view the full-screen effects

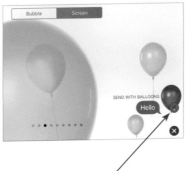

2 Tap once on this button to send the message

Quick replies (also known as Tapback)

It is possible to add a quick reply, in icon format. To do this:

1 Press and hold on the message to which you want to add a quick reply,

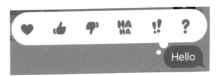

and tap once on one of the icons. This is sent to the recipient, attached to the original message

Adding photos and stickers

Photos, stickers and graphics can also be added to messages:

1 Tap once on this button next to the text box

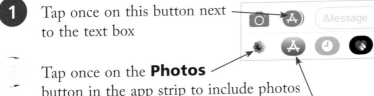

2 Tap once on the **Photos** button in the app strip to include photos in a message and tap once on the **Store** button to download sticker sets from the App Store

Having a Video Chat

Video chatting is a very personal and interactive way to keep in touch with family and friends around the world. The FaceTime app provides this facility with other iPad, iPhone and iPod Touch users, or a Mac computer with FaceTime. To use FaceTime for video chatting:

To make video calls with FaceTime you need an active internet connection and to be signed in with your Apple ID.

Skype and Zoom are other options for making free video calls to other Skype or Zoom users. The apps can be downloaded from the App Store.

NEW

When you receive a FaceTime call, it appears as a small banner at the top of the screen. This is known as a compact call and is a new feature with iPadOS 14.

116

1 Tap once on the **FaceTime** app

2 Recent video chats are shown under the Video tab. Tap once here to select a contact

Edit   +

FaceTime

3 Enter the name of a contact, or tap once on this button to select one from your Contacts app

New FaceTime   Cancel

To: | ⊕

4 Use the Contacts app to select a contact

Groups   **Contacts**   Cancel

Q Search   🎤

A

5 Tap once on the FaceTime video button to make a FaceTime call. The recipient must have FaceTime on their iPad, iPhone, iPod Touch or Mac computer

‹ Contacts

Eilidh

message   call   FaceTime   mail

6 Once you have selected a contact, FaceTime starts connecting with them, and their name or number appears at the top of the screen. If someone else makes a call to you, tap once on the red button to decline a call, or the green button to accept it

7 When you have connected, your contact appears in the main window and you appear in a Picture in Picture thumbnail in the corner

It is possible to silence incoming FaceTime calls and other alerts, at times when you do not want to be disturbed. This is done within the **Do Not Disturb** section in the **Settings** app. Drag the **Scheduled** button **On** to specify times during which you do not want to be disturbed. If required, calls from selected people can still be enabled via the **Allow Calls From** option, under the **Phone** heading.

8 Tap once on this button to take a Live Photo of the screen (this is a photo that is created as a small animation)

9 Use these buttons during a call to, from left to right: turn off the camera for the call (audio will still be available); mute  the microphone; switch the camera view on your iPad; and end the call. Swipe down on the top of the panel to hide these buttons

FaceTime can be used for group messaging, so numerous people can be included in the same FaceTime call. To do this, add each person to the call, following Steps 2-4 on the previous page.

Hot tip

On Facebook you can have private text conversations with your friends, as well as posting public information for all of your friends to see. For more information, check out **Facebook for Seniors in easy steps** in our online shop at www. ineasysteps.com

Beware

When you follow people on Twitter, their Tweets appear on your Homepage feed. If they are very prolific, or you follow a lot of people, this may result in a lot of messages to read. You can turn off notifications for individual apps if you wish – see page 142.

Communication Apps

Within the App Store there is a range of communication apps that can be used to contact friends and family via text, phone and video. There are also several apps for sharing information, updates and photos. Some of these are:

- **Facebook**. The social networking phenomenon that has over a billion users around the world. This app enables you to create and use a Facebook account from your iPad. You can then interact with friends and family by posting messages, comments and photos.

- **Twitter**. Another one of the top social networking sites on the web. It provides the facility to post text or news messages (Tweets) of up to 280 characters. You can choose other users to follow, so you see their Tweets, and other people can follow you to see yours, too.

- **Snapchat**. This is a popular photo- and video-sharing app: items can be shared for a limited period of time and they are then deleted.

- **Instagram**. Another very popular photo- and video-sharing app, used by people to document every part of their lives and activities.

- **Flickr**. An iPad version of the popular photo- and video-sharing site. You have to register for an account, and once you have done this you can share your photos and videos with a vast online community.

- **Skype**. The widely-used service for making video and voice calls. This is free when both users are using Skype over Wi-Fi. Skype can also be used for text messaging.

- **WordPress**. A web publishing app that can be used to create online blogs and your own websites.

- **Gmail**. If you have a Gmail account this will enable you to access it directly from your iPad.

- **Email Client App - myMail**. This can be used to access email from several web-based email services.

7 On a Web Safari

This chapter shows how to use the functionality of the built-in iPad web browser, Safari, to access the web and start enjoying the benefits of the online world.

Around Safari

The Safari app is the default web browser on the iPad. This can be used to view web pages, bookmark pages, and read pages with the Reader function. To start using Safari:

1 Tap once on the **Safari** app

2 Tap once on the Address Bar at the top of the Safari window. Type a name or a web page address

3 Tap once on the **Go** button on the keyboard to open the web page that was entered, or select one of the options below the Address Bar

4 The selected page opens with the top toolbar visible. As you scroll down the page, this disappears to give you a greater viewing area. Tap on the top of the screen, or scroll back up to display the toolbar again

Don't forget

The options below the Address Bar in Step 2 include: **Top Hits** for the item in the Address Bar; **Google Search**, which performs a search using the word or phrase entered into the Address Bar; or **Bookmarks and History**, which displays matching items from these locations in Safari.

Swipe up and down and left and right to navigate around the page

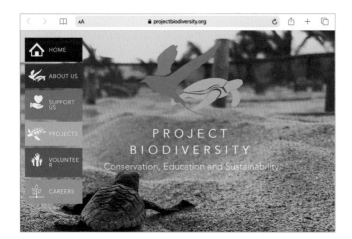

Swipe outwards with thumb and forefinger to zoom in on a web page (pinch inwards to zoom back out)

When a page opens in Safari, a blue status bar underneath the Address Bar indicates the progress of the loading page.

When a page opens in Safari, a blue status bar underneath the Address Bar indicates the progress of the loading page.

Double-tap with one finger to zoom in on a page by a set amount. Double-tap again with one finger to return to normal view. If the page has been zoomed by a greater amount by pinching, double-tap with two fingers to return to normal view.

Other browsers can be downloaded from the App Store. Some to try are: Google Chrome; Dolphin Web Browser; Firefox; and Opera Touch.

Safari Settings

Settings for Safari can be specified in the Settings app.

Beware

If other people have access to the iPad, don't use **AutoFill** for names and passwords for any sites with sensitive information, such as banking sites.

Hot tip

If the **Open New Tabs in Background** option in Step 4 is set to **On**, you can press and hold a link on a web page and select **Open in New Tab**. The link then opens in a new tab behind the one you are viewing.

Don't forget

Cookies are small items from websites that obtain details from your browser when you visit a site. The cookie remembers the details for the next time you visit the site.

1 Open the Settings app and tap once on the **Safari** tab

 Safari

2 Tap once on the **Search Engine** link to select a default search engine to use

Search Engine

3 Tap once here for options for filling in online forms

GENERAL
AutoFill

4 Drag this button **On** to open new pages in the background of your current page

Open New Tabs in Background

5 Drag this button **On** to keep the Favorites Bar in view under the Address Bar in Safari

Show Favorites Bar

6 Tap once on the **Block All Cookies** link to specify how Safari deals with cookies from websites

Block All Cookies

7 Tap once on **Clear History and Website Data** to remove these

Clear History and Website Data

8 Drag this button **On** to enable alerts for when you visit a fraudulent website

Fraudulent Website Warning

9 Drag this button **On** to block pop-up messages

Block Pop-ups

Navigating Pages

When you are viewing pages within Safari there are a number of functions that can be used:

1 Tap once on these arrows to move forward and back between web pages that have been visited

2 Tap once here to view bookmarked pages, Reading List pages and browsing history (see page 127)

3 Tap once here to add a bookmark (see page 127); add to a Reading List; add an icon to your iPad Home screen; email a link to a page; share using social media, messaging and other apps; or print a page

4 Tap once here to open a new tab (see page 125)

5 Tap and hold a link to access additional options, including: Open, Open in Background, Open in New Window, Download Linked File, Add to Reading List, Copy, or Share... using a selection of options

Open	⊘
Open in Background	⊞
Open in New Window	⊞
Download Linked File	⊙
Add to Reading List	∞
Copy	⧉
Share...	⬆

6 Tap and hold on an image, and tap once on **Share...**, **Add to Photos** or **Copy**

Share...	⬆
Add to Photos	⬇
Copy	⧉

Hot tip

Tap and hold on the **Forward** and **Back** arrows in Step 1 to view lists of previously-visited pages in these directions. See page 127 for more on bookmarking.

Hot tip

Files can be downloaded from Safari and then viewed in the Files app, from the Downloads button in the sidebar. To do this, press and hold on a link on a web page to the file you want to download, and tap once on the **Download Linked File** button.

Download Linked File	⊙

Web Page Options

Being able to view web pages in the way that you want is an important part of any browsing experience, and Safari offers various options for displaying web pages. These can be accessed from the left-hand side of the Address Bar:

In Reader View, the button in the Address Bar turns black. Tap once on it to access options for how Reader View is displayed, including text size, background color and font. It can also be used to hide Reader View and return to the full web page.

1 Tap once on this button in the Address Bar

2 The web page options are displayed

3 Tap once on these buttons to change the text size of a web page

124

4 Tap once on the **Show Reader View** button to view the current web page with just text and no extra content, such as adverts

5 Tap once on the **Hide Toolbar** button to hide the toolbar and create a larger viewing area for the current web page

Tap once on the **Privacy Report** button to view details of items that have been blocked.

6 Tap once on the **Request Mobile Website** button to view a mobile version of the website, if there is one

7 Tap once on the **Website Settings** button to access settings for the website being viewed

Opening New Tabs

Safari supports tabbed browsing, which means that you can open separate pages within the same window and access them by tapping on each tab at the top of the page:

1 Tap once here to open a new tab for another page

2 Open a new page by entering a web address into the Address Bar, or tap on one of the thumbnails in the **Favorites** window

3 Tap once on the tab headings to move between tabbed pages

4 Tap once on the cross to the top-left of a tab to close the active tab

Hot tip

The items that appear in the Favorites window can be determined within **Settings** > **Safari** by tapping once on the **Favorites** option.

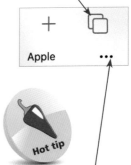
Don't forget

Press and hold on this button to access options for opening a new tab, opening a new private tab, or closing all of the currently-open tabs.

Hot tip

If there are too many items to be displayed on the Favorites Bar, tap once on this button to view the other items.

Tab View

Tabs can be managed using iPadOS 14 on the iPad so that you can view all of your open Safari tabs on one screen, including those on other compatible Apple devices. To do this:

Hot tip

Tab View can also be activated by pinching inwards with thumb and forefinger on a web page that is at normal magnification; i.e. 1 to 1.

Don't forget

Tap once on the **Done** button at the top of the Tab View window to exit this, and return to the web page that was being viewed when Tab View was activated.

1 Tap once here to activate **Tab View**

2 All of the currently-open tabs are displayed. Tap on one to open it

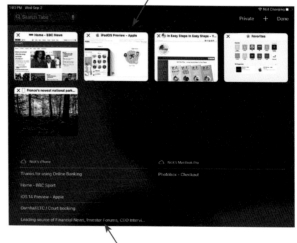

3 If you have open Safari tabs on other Apple devices, these will be shown at the bottom of the window

4 Tap once on this button at the top of the window to open another tab

5 Tap once on this button to open a **Private** tab, where no browsing history will be recorded during this browsing session

Bookmarking Pages

Once you start using Safari, you will soon build up a collection of favorite pages that you visit regularly. To access these quickly, they can be bookmarked so that you can go to them in one tap. To set up and use bookmarks:

1 Open a web page that you want to bookmark. Tap once here to access the sharing options

2 Tap once on the **Add Bookmark** button

3 Tap once in this box to select whether to include the bookmark on the Favorites Bar or in a Bookmarks folder

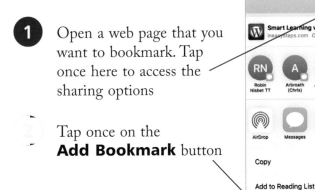

4 Tap once on the **Save** button

5 On the web page, tap once here to view all of the bookmarks. The Bookmarks folders are listed. Tap once on the **Edit** button at the bottom of the panel to delete or rename the folders

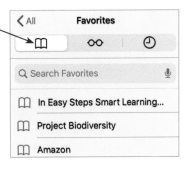

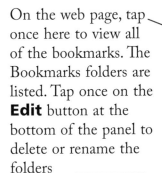

Hot tip

For pages that you access frequently, you can also choose to **Add to Home Screen** from the sharing options in Step 2 (swipe up the panel to access this option).

Don't forget

The button in Step 5 can also be used to access your Reading List and browsing history. Tap on this button to view your **Reading List**, for viewing offline.

Reading List items can be added from the Share button in Step 1.

Tap on this button to view your browsing history.

Apple Pay on the Web

Apple Pay is Apple's contactless payment system, which is activated using Touch ID on the iPad or the iPhone. On the iPhone it can be used to make purchases in hundreds of retail outlets, and also online with authorized websites. On the iPad it can only be used for online purchases. To do this:

Don't forget

To register a credit or debit card for Apple Pay, enter your name, card number, expiration date and security number. You will then be asked to confirm these details to activate the card. This will be done via a text message or phone call from your card provider, who will supply you with a number to activate the card. Once this is done, the card will be ready to use with Apple Pay.

1 Access **Settings > Touch ID & Passcode** and set up your iPad with both of these (see pages 20-21)

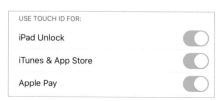
Touch ID & Passcode

2 Within **Touch ID & Passcode**, drag these buttons **On** for the items you want to use with Touch ID

USE TOUCH ID FOR:
iPad Unlock
iTunes & App Store
Apple Pay

3 Select **Settings > Wallet & Apple Pay**

Wallet & Apple Pay

4 Tap once on the **Add Credit or Debit Card** button

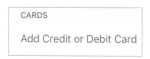
CARDS
Add Credit or Debit Card

5 Complete the Apple Pay wizard for the selected credit or debit card (see tip). Once a card has been registered, it can be used to purchase items from participating websites where you see this symbol, or from the iTunes and App Stores, if specified, as in Step 2. Press the **Home** button to buy an item with Touch ID

 Pay

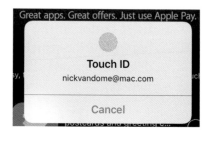
Great apps. Great offers. Just use Apple Pay.
Touch ID
nickvandome@mac.com
Cancel

8 Staying Organized

Taking Notes

It is always useful to have a quick way of making notes of everyday things, such as shopping lists, recipes or packing lists. On your iPad, the Notes app is perfect for this:

The Notes app has been updated in iPadOS 14.

1 Tap once on the **Notes** app

2 Tap once on this button to create a new note

If iCloud is set up for Notes (check **Notes** is **On** in **Settings** > **Apple ID** > **iCloud**) then all of your notes will be stored here and will be available on any other iCloud-enabled devices that you have.

3 Tap once in the text area of a new note to access the keyboard. Start writing the note

Formatting notes

To apply a range of formatting to a note:

1 Press and hold next to the piece of text you want to format. Tap once on the **Select** button

The title for a note is taken from the first line of text that is entered.

2 Drag the yellow selection handles over the text you want to select

3 Tap once on the **Formatting** button on the Shortcuts bar to access the formatting options, including text styles such as the Title, Heading or Body options, or list options for creating a list from the selection

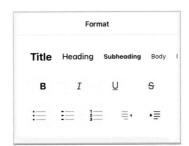

Options for formatting text in a note are located on the Shortcuts bar, below the main text window, and on the top toolbar.

4 Tap once on the **List** button on the top toolbar to create a checklist from the selected text. Radio buttons are added to the list (these are the round buttons to the left-hand side of the text). Tap once on the radio buttons to show that an item or a task has been completed

Items in a list can be set to automatically move to the bottom of the list once they have been completed. To do this, go to **Settings** > **Notes** > **Sort Checked Items** and tap once on the **Automatically** option.

5 Tap once on the **Camera** button on the top toolbar and tap once on the **Take Photo or Video** button to add a photo or a video to the note, or tap once on the **Choose Photo or Video** button to add a photo from the iPad's photo library

Tap once on this button on the Shortcuts bar to insert a table into a note.

131

...cont'd

Hot tip

Tap once on the menu button in the top right-hand corner of the Notes panel to access a menu for managing your notes, including: changing the notes window view; selecting notes; sorting notes; and viewing any attachments that have been added to notes.

Hot tip

Notes can also be deleted by swiping from right to left on them in the Notes panel and tapping once on the Trash icon.

6 Tap once on the **Add Sketch** button to add a freehand sketch to a note. Click on the pen and color options as required

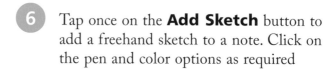

7 Tap once on this button on the keyboard to hide the keyboard and finish the note. To edit an existing note, tap once on the text and the keyboard will reappear

Managing notes

Once notes have been created they can be managed from within their own window. To do this:

1 In the main notes window, tap once on the menu button, at the right-hand side of the top toolbar

2 Tap once on the menu options to apply them. These include options for: scanning items into a note; pinning a note; locking a note; or deleting it. There are also options for: sharing the current note; searching for items; moving a note to a folder within the Notes app; and applying lines and grids over a note

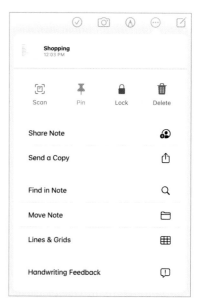

Pinning notes

By default, the most recently-created, or edited, note appears at the top of the Notes panel. However, it is possible to pin your most frequently-used notes to the top of this panel. To do this:

1 Press and hold on the note to be pinned

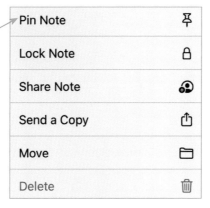

The function of pinning notes in the Notes app is a new feature in iPadOS 14.

2 Tap once on the **Pin Note** button

Pin Note	📌
Lock Note	🔒
Share Note	👥
Send a Copy	⬆️
Move	📂
Delete	🗑️

3 The note is pinned at the top of the Notes panel. Tap once here to show, or hide, the pinned notes

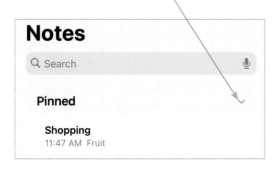

To unpin a note, press and hold on it and tap once on the **UnPin Note** button.

...cont'd

Copy as text with the Apple Pencil

The Apple Pencil can be used to create handwritten text within a note. This can then also be converted into typed text and copied into other apps, if required. To do this:

Adding handwritten text to a note with the Apple Pencil and converting it to typed text is a new feature in iPadOS 14.

1 Tap once on this button to create a new note

2 Write the required text with the Apple Pencil

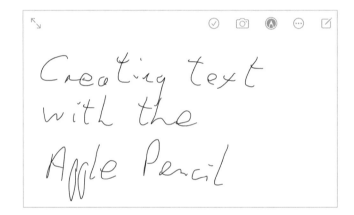

134

Once handwritten text has been selected, it can then be moved around, by pressing and dragging on the selected item.

3 Double-tap on a word with a finger to select it

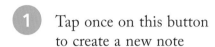
Delete   Duplicate   Copy as Text   Insert Space Above

4 Drag the yellow selection handles to select the required text. Tap once on the selected text

5 Tap once on the **Copy as Text** button `Copy as Text`

6 Open a new note (or another app such as the Mail app), tap in a blank text area, and tap once on the **Paste** button to paste the copied text as typed text

The **Copy as Text** button in Step 5 is part of the toolbar that appears when you tap on a piece of selected text.

Creating shapes

Freehand shapes can also be drawn with the Apple Pencil in a note, and then be converted into a graphical shape:

1 Draw a freehand shape with the Apple Pencil and double-tap on it with your finger to select it

The Snap to Shape function is a new feature in iPadOS 14.

2 Tap once on the **Snap to Shape** button `Snap to Shape`

3 The drawing is converted into a graphical shape

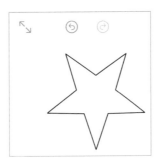

135

Setting Reminders

Another useful organization app is Reminders. This enables you to create lists for different topics and then set reminders for specific items. A date and time can be set for each reminder, and when this is reached the reminder appears on your iPad screen. To use Reminders:

Hot tip

Reminders is one of the apps that can also be used with the online iCloud service, which is provided once you have an Apple ID. This is accessed at **www.icloud.com** Other apps that can be accessed here include Contacts, Calendar and Notes.

Hot tip

If Family Sharing has been set up (see page 71 for details) you can create a family reminder that will appear for all members in your Family Sharing circle. To do this, tap once on the **Family** button in Step 2 and add a reminder in the usual way.

1 Tap once on the **Reminders** app

2 The items that have been created are listed under specific categories and beneath the **My Lists** heading. This includes reminders and lists. Tap once on the **Edit** button to reorder or delete any of the lists

3 Tap once on the Reminders option and tap once on the **New Reminder** button

4 Enter details of the reminder and tap once on the **i** button to access the **Details** window

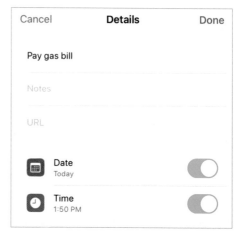

5 Drag the **Date** or **Time** buttons **On** and select options for the relevant options for the reminder

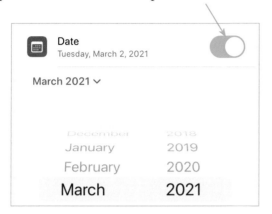

6 Tap once on the **Done** button to create the reminder

7 On the date and time of the reminder, a pop-up box appears. Press on the reminder to expand the box. Tap once on

Mark as Completed to close the reminder, or select an option for being reminded about it

8 Tap once on the **Today** and **Scheduled** buttons at the

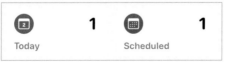

top left-hand side of the main app window shown in Step 2 on the previous page to see reminders and lists for these categories. Appropriate items will be added automatically to these categories

Hot tip

For a recurring reminder, tap once on the **Repeat** link in the **Details** window (if a date and time have been set) and select a repeat option from: Never, Hourly, Daily, Weekly, Biweekly, Monthly, Every 3 Months, Every 6 Months, or Yearly. The reminder will then appear at the specified time and date set in Step 5.

Using the Calendar

The built-in iPad calendar can be used to create and view appointments and events. To do this:

The iPad calendar uses continuous scrolling to move through Month view. This means you can view weeks across different months, rather than just viewing each month in its entirety; i.e. you can view the second half of one month and the first half of the next one in the same calendar window.

1 Tap once on the **Calendar** app

2 By default, the calendar is displayed in **Month** view. Swipe up and down to move between the weeks and months

138

3 Tap once here to view the calendar by **Day**, **Week**, **Month** or **Year** view

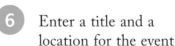

4 Tap once on the **Today** button to view the current date **Today**

5 Tap once on this button to create a new event, or press and hold on a different date to add an event here ＋

Drag the **All-day** button **On** to set the event for the whole day.

All-day ⦿

6 Enter a title and a location for the event

7 Drag the **All-day** button from **On** to **Off** to set a timescale for the event

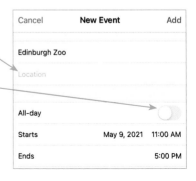

8 Tap on the **Starts** and **Ends** dates to set these

9 To invite other people to the event, tap once on the **Invitees** link (Calendars needs to be **On** in iCloud for this function)

10 Tap once on this button to select a contact from your address book

11 The contact is added as an invitee for the event

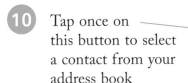

12 Tap once on the **Done** button. An email invitation will then be sent to the invitee's email address

13 Tap once on the **Add** button in Step 8 when you have finished entering the details of the event

14 Press and hold on an event, and tap on the **Edit** button to alter the details for the event

Hot tip

A new event can also be created in **Day** view. Press and hold on a time slot to access the **New Event** window.

Hot tip

Tap once on the **Repeat** link in the **New Event** window to set a recurring event, such as a birthday. The repeat options are Every Day, Every Week, Every 2 Weeks, Every Month, or Every Year.

Don't forget

Select an event to edit as in Step 14, and tap once on the **Delete Event** button at the bottom of the window to remove it.

Delete Event

Your iPad Address Book

There is a built-in address book on your iPad: the Contacts app. This enables you to store contact details, which can then be used to contact people via email, iMessage or FaceTime. To add contacts:

1 Tap once on the **Contacts** app

2 Tap once on this button to add a new contact

3 Enter the required details for a contact

Don't forget

The details of an individual contact can be shared via email or as an iMessage, using the **Share Contact** button at the bottom of their entry.

Share Contact

4 Tap once on the **Done** button Done

5 Use these buttons to send a text message, make a call, start a FaceTime video call or send an email to the contact

6 Tap once on the **Edit** button to edit details in an individual entry Edit

7 To delete a contact, swipe to the bottom of the window in Edit mode and tap once on the **Delete Contact** button Delete Contact

Printing Items

Printing from an iPad has advantages and disadvantages. One advantage is that it is done wirelessly, so you do not have to worry about connecting wires and cables to a printer. The main disadvantage is that not all printers work with the iPad printing system.

AirPrint

Content from an iPad is printed using the AirPrint system that is part of the iPadOS 14 operating system. This is a wireless printing system that connects to your printer through your Wi-Fi network. However, not all printers are AirPrint- or Wi-Fi-enabled, so it may not work with your current printer.

AirPrint can print content from apps with the Share button, including built-in apps like Safari, Notes, Mail, and Photos:

Check on the Apple website for a list of AirPrint-enabled printers: **https:// support.apple.com/ en-us/HT201311**

1. Tap once on the **Share** button and tap once on the **Print** button

Print

2. Tap once on **Select Printer** to select your AirPrint printer

3. Select options for the number of copies, double- or single-sided, and color, then tap once on the **Print** button

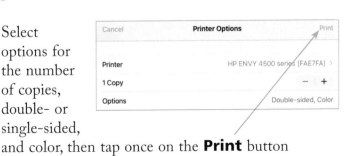

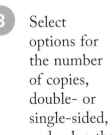

Apps in the Apple productivity suite – Pages, Numbers and Keynote – contain the **Print** button within the **More** options that are accessed from the top toolbar.

Keeping Notified

Although the Notification Center feature is not an app in its own right, it can be used to display information from a variety of apps. The notifications appear as a list of all of the items you want to be reminded about or be made aware of. Notifications are set up within the Settings app. To do this:

1 Tap once on the **Settings** app

2 Tap once on the **Notifications** tab

3 In the **Notification Style** section, tap on an item to determine how it operates when it displays a notification

Hot tip

At the bottom of the window in Step 5 there is a **Notification Grouping** option. Set this to **Automatic**, so that all similar notifications are grouped together.

4 Drag the **Allow Notifications** button **On** to allow notifications to be displayed for this item

5 Make selections for how you want the notification to appear. This includes the Lock screen, the Notification Center and as an onscreen banner

Viewing notifications

Once the Notifications settings have been selected, they can be used to keep up-to-date with all of your important appointments and reminders, via the Notification Center. To view the Notification Center:

1 Drag down from the top of any screen to view the Notification Center. This displays items that have been selected as shown on the previous page. Tap once on an item to open it in its own app

2 On the Home screen, swipe from left to right to view the Today View panel, where apps with date-specific information, such as the Calendar and Reminders apps, can be displayed

Don't forget

For more details about working with the Today View panel, see pages 34-41.

Organization Apps

In the App Store there is a wide range of productivity and organization apps. Some of these are:

- **Evernote**. One of the most popular note-taking apps. You can create individual notes and also save them into notebook folders. Evernote works across multiple devices, so if it is installed on other computers or mobile devices, you can access your notes wherever you are.

- **Popplet**. This is a note-taking app that enables you to link notes together, so you can form a mindmap-type creation. You can also include photos and draw pictures.

- **Dropbox**. This is an online service for storing and accessing files. You can upload files from your iPad and then access them from other devices with an internet connection.

- **Bamboo Paper**. This is another note-taking app, but it allows you to do this by handwriting rather than typing. The free version comes with one notebook into which you can put your notes, and the paid-for version provides another 20.

- **Pages**. This is a powerful word processing app that has been developed by Apple. It can be used to create and save documents, which can then be printed or shared via email. There are a number of templates on which documents can be based. There is also a range of formatting and content options.

- **Keynote**. Another Apple productivity app, this is a presentation app that can be used to create slides, which can then be run as a presentation.

- **Numbers**. This is the spreadsheet app that is part of the same suite as Pages and Keynote. Again, templates are provided, or you can create your spreadsheets from scratch to keep track of expenditure or household bills. You can enter formulas into cells to perform simple or complicated calculations.

Most organization apps are found in the **Productivity** category of the App Store.

Other productivity and organization apps to look at include: Notability; Alarmed; AnyList: Grocery Shopping List; OfficeSuite; iA Writer; Smartsheet; and GoodReader PDF Editor & Viewer.

9 Like a Good Book

Your iPad can be used for getting the news, and reading a wide array of books.

Getting the News

The News app is a news-aggregation app that collates news stories from a variety of publications, covering a range of categories. To use the News app:

1 Tap once on the **News** app

2 Tap once on the **Today** button in the sidebar to view the current news stories

3 The current news stories, based on your news feed, are displayed in the main window

4 Tap once on the **Edit** button to the right of the **Search** box

5 Your current news feed items can be removed by tapping on the red circle next to them. The order of importance can be rearranged by dragging these buttons. Tap once on the **Done** button

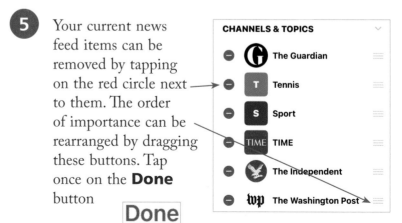

Hot tip

Tap once on this icon to show, or hide, the sidebar.

...cont'd

6 Scroll to the bottom of the left-hand panel, as displayed in Step 3 on the previous page, and tap once on the **Discover Channels & Topics** button

Hot tip

Below the **Channels & Topics** heading in Step 3 is a **Suggested By Siri** heading that contains topics based on Siri searches. Tap once on the **+** icon to add a topic to your news feed.

Discover Channels & Topics

7 Suggested channels and topics are displayed. These can be added to your news feed by tapping once on the **+** icon next to an item. Tap once on the **Done** button

8 Tap once on a news item in Step 3 on the previous page to view it in detail

Don't forget

Scroll down the **Follow Your Favorites** page to view more topics.

9 When an item has been opened for reading, tap on these buttons on the top toolbar to, from left to right: change the text size of an article; bookmark an item; or share the item (or save it) to specific people, via the Messages app, or via Mail

Hot tip

Tap once on these arrows to move between the next and previous news stories.

147

Hot tip

Check out other **In Easy Steps** books in the Apple Book Store!

The **Browse Sections** option in the Book Store contains links to a range of options, including **New & Trending**, **Top Charts**, **Bestsellers** and **Rave Reviews**. Tap on a category to view its content.

Don't forget

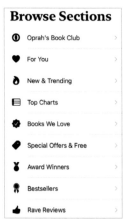

Finding Books

For anyone interested in reading, the iPad removes the need to carry around a lot of bulky books. Whether you are at home or traveling, you can keep hundreds of digital books (ebooks) on your iPad. This is done with the Books app, which can be used to download and read books across most genres, like a portable library. To use Books:

1 Tap once on the **Books** app

2 The Books app opens at the **Reading Now** section, which consists of any items that you have downloaded, and suggested titles

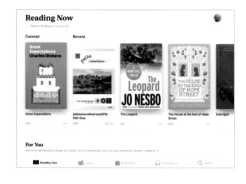

3 Tap once on the **Book Store** button on the bottom toolbar to access titles that can be bought and downloaded to the Books app (see next page)

4 Tap once on the **Browse Sections** button in the top left-hand corner of the Book Store Homepage to view items according to different categories (see tip)

Downloading Books

Once you have identified appropriate books in the Book Store, they can then be downloaded to the **Library** section of the Books app. To do this:

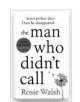

1 Tap once on the book image or title to view its details

2 View the details of the book, including a description. Scroll down the page to view more details about the book

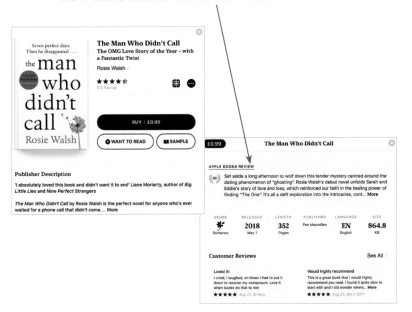

3 Tap once on the **Buy** (or **Get**) button to purchase and download the book. Downloaded books appear in the **Library** section of the Books app. Tap once on the **Want To Read** button to add the book as a suggested item under the Reading Now section. Tap once on the **Sample** button to read a sample directly from the Book Store, without downloading it

Reading Books

Reading an Apple book

Once you have opened an Apple book, there are a number of ways to navigate and work with the content:

Hot tip

To hide the toolbar, tap once on a page.

Don't forget

The Table of Contents can be used to view bookmarks and notes (see next page) that have been added to pages. From the Table of Contents page, tap once on the **Resume** button to return to the page you were looking at.

Don't forget

If you are viewing a sample version of a book, there is a **Buy** button on the top toolbar. Tap once on this to buy the full version of the book.

1 Tap once in the middle of a page in an Apple book to access the top toolbar

2 Tap once on this button to return to the Books **Library** (bookcase)

3 Tap once on this button to view the Table of Contents

Great Expectations			Resume
Contents	Bookmarks	Notes	
Great Expectations			1
Chapter I			2
Chapter II			14
Chapter III			35
Chapter IV			47

4 Tap once on this button to change the text size, font or color

5 Tap once on this button to search for an item in the book

6 Tap once on this button to bookmark a page

7 Drag on this bottom bar to move through the book

Back to page 14   140 of 1159

Working with text

When you are reading an Apple book there are a number of options for enhancing the reading experience, from looking up dictionary definitions of words to making notes about the text. To do this:

1 Press and hold on a word to highlight it and access the text toolbar

2 Tap once on the **Look Up** button to access a dictionary definition for the selected word, and suggested related websites, videos and apps. At the bottom of the window there is also an option for searching over the web

3 Highlight a word and drag on each of the blue markers to extend the highlighted area

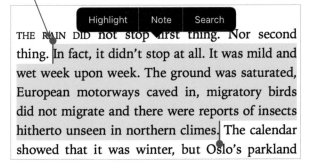

Tap once on the **Search** button in Step 1 to see where a selected word or phrase appears throughout the book.

If you click on one of the suggestions in Step 2, this takes you away from the Apple book page.

Tap once on the **Note** button in Step 3 to add a note about the selected text.

Tap once on the **Highlight** button in Step 3 to highlight the selected text with a specific color.

Kindle on your iPad

The Kindle is a popular eReader device for reading ebooks. It is possible to use the Kindle app on your iPad to download Kindle books to it:

1 Download the Kindle app from the Books category in the App Store and tap once on it to open it

2 If you have an Amazon account, enter the details here to register the Kindle app through your iPad. If you do not have an Amazon account, one can be obtained from the Amazon website

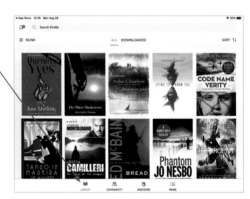

Hot tip

Once a book has been downloaded, it can be removed from your iPad by pressing on it in the **Downloaded** section and tapping once on the **Remove from Device** button.

3 Tap once on the **Library** button on the bottom toolbar to view the titles that are in the Kindle Cloud; i.e. in your Kindle account on Amazon.

Tap once on one to download it to your iPad

4 Tap once on the **Downloaded** tab to view the available titles

5 Tap once on the **Discover** button on the bottom toolbar to search for more Kindle titles

10 Leisure Time

The possibilities for enjoyment from your iPad are huge. This chapter looks at listening to music and capturing and editing photos. It also covers some lifestyle apps including art, health, cookery and games.

Buying Music and More

As well as using the Music app (see pages 156-157), music on the iPad can also be accessed using the iTunes Store, using your Apple ID with credit or debit card details added. Music can then be played via the Music app:

1 Tap once on the **iTunes Store** app

2 Tap once on the **Music** button on the iTunes toolbar at the bottom of the window

Music can also be found, and previewed, from the **Browse** button in the **Music** app. Items can then be bought by tapping once on the **Buy on iTunes Store** button.

154

3 Scroll up and down to view the featured items, or tap once on the **Genres** button to find items this way

4 Tap once on an item to view it. Tap once here to buy an album, or tap on the price button next to a song to buy that individual item

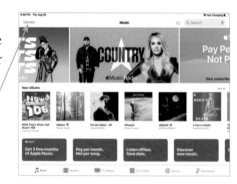

5 Purchased items are included in the Music app's Library (see pages 156-157) as well as the iTunes Library, from where they can be downloaded again at any time to your iPad or any other Apple device

Around the iTunes Store

In addition to music, there is a wide range of other content that can be downloaded from the iTunes Store:

1 Tap once on the **Movies** button to view the latest movie releases

2 Tap once on the **TV Shows** button to view the latest TV releases

3 Tap once on the **Top Charts** button on the bottom toolbar to view the top-selling items for music, movies and TV

4 Tap once on the **Genius** button on the bottom toolbar to view suggestions made by iTunes based on your previous purchases

5 Tap once on the **Purchased** button on the bottom toolbar to view all of your previous purchases from the iTunes Store

Don't forget

Scroll up and down to view the content on the Homepage for Movies and TV. Swipe left and right on individual panels to view the items in each section. Tap once on the **See All** button at the top of a panel – e.g. Recent Releases – to view all of the items within it.

155

Hot tip

Since all items that you buy and download from the iTunes Store are kept within the Purchased section, if you ever delete or lose an item you can download it again, for free, from this section. Tap once on the cloud icon next to an item to download it again.

Hot tip

To create a playlist of songs, tap once on the **Playlists** button in the left-hand panel, then tap once on the **New Playlist** button. Give it a name, and then you can add songs from your Library.

Playlists

Hot tip

Another music option is Apple Music. This is a subscription service that makes the entire Apple iTunes library of music available to users. Music can be streamed over the internet, or downloaded so you can listen to it when you are offline. Apple Music can be accessed from the **Listen Now** button in the left-hand panel of the Music app.

Playing Music

Once music has been bought from the iTunes Store, it can be played on your iPad using the Music app. To do this:

1. Tap once on the **Music** app

2. Tap once on the **Library** button in the left-hand panel

3. Tap once on the **Library** button in the top left-hand corner. Select one of the options for viewing items in the Library. This can be **Recently Added**, **Artists**, **Albums**, **Songs** or **Genres**

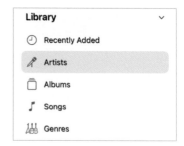

4. For the **Artists** section, tap once on an artist in the left-hand panel to view the related items in the right-hand panel

5. Tap once on an item in the right-hand panel to view its details. The tracks from the album are displayed

6 Tap once on a track to play it.
Limited options for the music controls are displayed at the bottom of the window. Tap here to view details of a track

7 The details of the track are displayed. Use these buttons to rewind, pause/play and fast-forward the track

8 Tap once on this button to access the menu for the currently-playing track. This includes sharing the song, downloading it onto your iPad, deleting it, adding it to a playlist, or sharing it

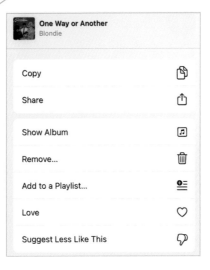

Hot tip

Tap once on the **Browse** button in the left-hand sidebar to preview music from the iTunes Store. Items can then be bought from the iTunes Store, if required, from a link in the Browse section.

Don't forget

By default, music that has been bought from the iTunes Store is kept online and can be played on your iPad by streaming it online over Wi-Fi. However, it is also possible to download tracks to your iPad so that you can play them without being online. Tap once on this button to download a track:

157

The camera on the back of the iPad is capable of capturing high-resolution photos and also high-definition videos. The front-facing one is better for video calls and "selfies" (photos of yourself).

If you do not want to take a Live Photo, make sure that the button in Step 4 is **Off**.

Photos can also be taken with the Camera app by pressing either of the **Volume** buttons on the side of the iPad.

Taking Photos and Videos

The iPad is excellent for taking and displaying photos. Photos can be captured directly using one of the two built-in cameras (one on the front and one on the back) and then viewed, edited and shared using the Photos app.

1   Tap once on the **Camera** app

2   Tap once on the shutter button to capture a photo

3   Tap once on this button to swap between the front and back cameras on the iPad

4   Tap once on this button on the top camera toolbar to take a Live Photo, which is a short animated video, in GIF file format. Live Photos can be played in the Photos app by pressing and holding on them to view the animated effects

The main iPad camera can be used for different formats:

1   Swipe up or down at the side of the camera screen, to access the shooting options. Tap once on the **Photo** button to capture photos at full-screen size. Tap once on the **Square** button to capture photos at this ratio. Tap once on the **Pano** button (accessed by scrolling past the Square option) to create panorama shots

VIDEO

• PHOTO

SQUARE

2   Tap once on the **Video** button in Step 1, and press the red shutter button to take a video. Press the shutter button again to stop recording

Photos Settings

iCloud sharing

Certain photo options can be applied within Settings. Several of these are to do with storing and sharing your photos via iCloud. To access these:

1 Tap once on the **Settings** app

2 Tap once on the **Photos** tab

3 Drag the **iCloud Photos** button

On to upload your whole photo Library from your iPad to the iCloud (it remains on your iPad too). Similarly, photos on your other Apple devices can also be uploaded to the iCloud

4 Select an option for storing iCloud photos

(**Optimize iPad Storage** uses less storage as it uses smaller file sizes of your images on your iPad, although the original file sizes are retained in iCloud)

5 Drag the **Upload to My Photo Stream** button **On** to enable photos and videos from the last 30 days to be uploaded automatically to the iCloud, via Wi-Fi

6 Drag the **Shared Albums** button **On** to enable

sharing your albums with family and friends, and also to be able to see their shared albums

In the **Camera** settings, drag the **Grid** button **On** to place a grid over the screen when you are taking photos with the camera, if required. This can be used to help compose photos by placing subjects using the grid.

Viewing Photos

Photos section

Photos can be viewed and organized in the Photos app. There are different sections for displaying photos in different ways. All photos can be viewed in the Photos section:

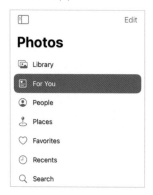

1 Tap once on the **Photos** app

2 Tap once on this button in the top left-hand corner of the Photos app to show, or hide, the sidebar

3 Tap once on the **Library** button in the sidebar and tap once on the **Years**, **Months**, **Days** or **All Photos** buttons to view your photos according to these criteria

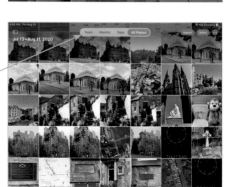

4 In any of the categories, double-tap on a photo to view it at full size

For You section

The For You section is where the best of your photos are selected and displayed automatically. To use this:

1 Tap once on the **For You** button on the sidebar

2 The **For You** section contains **Memories**, **Featured Photos**, and **Shared Albums**

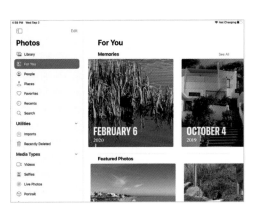

3 Memories are collections of photos created by the Photos app, using what it determines are the best shots for a related series of photos

4 Tap once on this button to play a Memory slideshow, with transitions between the photos and music

Hot tip

When a Memory is playing as a full-screen slideshow (from the button in Step 4) tap once on an image on the screen and tap once on the **Edit** button in the top right-hand corner to access the editing options for the Memory. These include editing the music, title, duration and the items in the Memory. Tap once on the **Done** button in the top right-hand corner to exit the editing mode.

...cont'd

Albums section

Albums can also be created to store similar photos:

Photos can be selected to enable options to be applied to them, such as being added to an album. To do this, access Days or All Photos in the Library section and tap once on the **Select** button. Tap on the photos you want to select, or drag over a range of photos.

1 Access the **My Albums** section within the sidebar

2 Tap once on the **New Album** button at the bottom of the My Albums section

3 Enter a name for the new album and tap once on the **Save** button

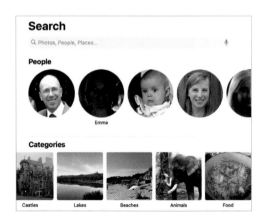

4 Tap once on the photos to be added to the album, and tap once on the **Done** button in the top right-hand corner of the window

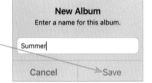

Shared albums can be created in a similar way to standard ones. To do this, access the **Shared Albums** section in the sidebar and tap once on the **New Shared Album** button. Enter the name for the album and then invite people to view it, so it becomes shared. Photos can then be added to the album.

Search options

Items can be searched for in the Photos app by tapping once on the **Search** button in the sidebar. Suggested areas are displayed. Tap once on an item to see the photos within it, or enter a keyword or phrase into the Search box to search for specific items.

Editing Photos

The Photos app has options to perform a range of photo-editing operations. To use these:

1 Open a photo at full-screen size and tap once on the **Edit** button in the top right-hand corner

2 The main editing buttons are located on the left-hand side of the screen. These are for, from top to bottom: color adjustment, filters, and rotation and cropping

3 Tap once on one of the main editing buttons to view its options at the right-hand side of the screen

4 For the **Adjust** options, each item has a slider that can be used to change the level of the color adjustment

5 The **Filter** option has a range of filter effects at the right-hand side of the screen. Tap once on one of these to apply it to the photo

6 For the **Rotate** option, there are choices for how to rotate a photo; e.g. horizontally or vertically

7 Tap once on the **Done** button in the top right-hand corner to apply any editing changes that have been made

Don't forget

The color options in the Adjust section include: Auto, Exposure, Brilliance, Contrast, Brightness, Saturation, and Tint.

Hot tip

The **Photo Booth** app is a good one to use with grandchildren, who will enjoy experimenting with its fun and special effects. Open the app, select one of the effects, and take the photo as normal.

Photo Booth

Viewing Movies and TV Shows

The TV app can be used to download and view movies and TV shows from the Apple TV service. There is no subscription for using the TV app on the iPad, but individual items usually require a payment, to buy or rent.

If you rent videos from the TV app you have to watch them within 30 days. Once you have started watching a video, you have to finish watching it within 48 hours. Once the rental period has expired, the video is deleted from the iPad.

Don't forget

The TV app can also be used to access the Apple TV+ service. This is a subscription service for streaming original TV shows and movies from Apple TV. There is a 7-day free trial and then the service costs $4.99 a month in the US and £4.99 in the UK.

164

1 Tap once on the **TV** app

2 Tap once on the **Watch Now** button on the bottom toolbar. Options for 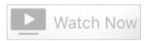 accessing the available content are displayed. Swipe up and down the page to view the content and tap once on the **See All** button to view all of the items within a category

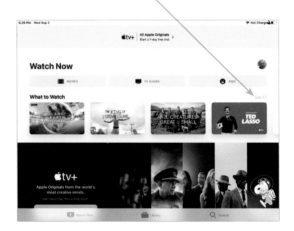

3 Tap once on the **Movies**, **TV Shows**  and **Kids** buttons at the top of the window to view items in these categories and download them

4 Tap once on the **Library** button on the bottom toolbar to view all of the items that you have downloaded from the TV app

Art and Drawing

Viewing art

It is always a pleasure to view works of art in real life, but the next-best alternative is to be able to look at them on the high-resolution Retina Display on your iPad. As far as viewing art goes, there are two options:

- Using apps that contain general information about museums and art galleries.

- Using apps that display the works belonging to museums and art galleries.

In general, type the name of a museum or art gallery into the App Store Search box to see if there is an applicable app.

Creating pictures

If you want to branch out from just looking at works of art, you can try creating some of your own too. There are a range of drawing and painting apps that can be used to let your creative side run riot. Most of these function in a similar fashion in terms of creating pictures, with drawing tools that you can select and then use to create a drawing by using your finger on the screen (or an Apple Pencil). Most drawing apps also have an Undo function and an Eraser to remove unwanted items. Some apps to try are:

- **Brushes Redux**. One of the most powerful painting apps with a wide range of tools and features, including up to six layers in each painting and five blend modes.

- **Drawing Pad**. Similar to Brushes Redux, but not at such a high level. Suitable as a starter option for iPad painting.

- **Inspire Pro**. A wide range of blending features makes this one of the best painting apps around.

- **How to Draw Everything**. A drawing app that has tutorials for learning how to draw, and also examples that can be used as templates and copied over.

- **Sketch.Book – Draw, Drawing Pad**. A sketching app at a similar level to Brushes Redux, for painting.

Most top museums have some form of app available. If there is not one for a museum in which you are interested, try contacting the museum and ask if they are planning on developing an app.

If you cannot find a certain app in the search results in the App Store, tap once on the **Filters** button, to the left of the Search box, and select the **Supports > iPhone Only** option. These apps can be downloaded for the iPad too, although they will have a smaller screen area to view the app.

If you are using your iPad in the kitchen, keep it away from direct contact with cooking areas, to avoid splashes and possible damage. If there is a risk of this, cover the iPad with clingfilm/plastic wrap to give it some protection.

Many recipe apps have a facility for uploading your own recipes, so that they can be shared with other people.

Cooking with your iPad

Your iPad may not be quite clever enough to cook dinner for you, but there are enough cookery apps to ensure that you will never go without a good meal with your iPad at your side. Some to look at are:

- **Allrecipes Magazine.** Packed full of recipes, step-by-step guides and cooking ideas, from the world's largest online community of chefs.

- **Change4Life Smart Recipes.** Over 160 healthy and tasty recipes for all meals throughout the day. There are also options for creating shopping lists and saving favorite recipes that you have created.

- **BigOven Recipes & Meal Planner.** Over 350,000 recipes to keep you busy in the kitchen for as long as you want. You can also store your grocery lists here.

- **Cake Recipes.** To get your mouth watering, this app has hundreds of cake ideas, from the simple to the exotic.

- **Green Kitchen.** A must for vegetarians, with stylish and creative recipes for organic and vegetarian food.

- **Jamie's Recipes.** An app featuring the recipes of the well-known chef Jamie Oliver. (Most well-known chefs now have their own cooking apps: just enter the name of a chef in the App Store to see the options.)

- **Healthy Slow Cooker Recipes.** Put your dish together with this app, leave it in the slow cooker, and then enjoy it several hours later when ready.

Staying Healthy

Most people are more health-conscious these days, and usefully the App Store has a category covering Health & Fitness. This includes apps about general fitness, healthy eating, relaxation and yoga. Some to try are:

- **MyFitnessPal**. If you want to stick to a diet, this app can help you along the way. You need to register, which is free, and then you can set your own diet plan and fitness profile.

- **Daily Workouts Fitness Trainer**. Some of the exercise apps are for dedicated gym-goers. If you are looking for something a bit less extreme, this app could fit the bill. A range of easy-to-follow exercises that will keep you fit.

- **Daily Yoga: Weight Loss Studio**. Audio and video instructions for timed sessions, and over 30 yoga poses.

- **Meal Planner Pal**. A dieting aid that enables you to create your own menu plans.

- **My Pilates Guru Lite**. Use this app to work through over 80 Pilates exercise sessions. You can also create your own sessions and save them to repeat.

- **Relax Melodies: Sleep Sounds**. Over 50 sound files to help you relax or fall asleep. Different melodies can be combined to create a customized soundtrack to help you get to sleep.

Mix 100+ sounds, meditations and bedtime stories

- **Sleep Pillow White Noise Sound**. Everyone enjoys a good night's sleep, and this app can help you achieve it with a collection of ambient soothing sounds.

- **Universal Breathing**. Designed to promote slow breathing, to enhance relaxation and general health.

There is also a **Medical** category in the App Store that contains a range of apps covering varied medical topics and subjects.

The iPhone also has a built-in **Health** app. However, this is not provided with the iPad, as it is designed to work with the iPhone and the Apple Watch. Find out more in our companion book iPhone & Apple Watch for Health & Fitness in easy steps.

If you have a genuine medical complaint, get it checked out by your doctor, rather than searching online.

Playing Games

Although computer games may seem like the preserve of the younger generation, this is definitely not the case. Not all computer games are of the shoot-em-up or racing variety, and the App Store also contains puzzles and versions of popular board games. Some games to try are:

- **Chess**. Pit your wits against this Chess app. Various settings can be applied for each game, such as the level of difficulty.

- **Checkers**. Similar to the Chess app, but for Checkers (Draughts). Hints are also available to help develop your skills and knowledge.

- **Mahjong**. A version of the popular Chinese game, this is a matching game for single players, rather than playing with other people.

- **Scrabble GO**. An iPad version of the best-selling word game that can be played with up to four people.

- **Solitaire**. An old favorite, the card game where you have to build sequences and remove all of the cards.

- **Sudoku**. The logic game where you have to fill different grids with numbers 1-9, without having any of the same number in a row or column.

- **Tetris**. One of the original computer games, where you have to piece together falling shapes to make lines.

- **Words With Friends**. Similar to Scrabble, an online word game, played with other users.

Don't forget

As well as the games here, there is a full range of other types of games in the App Store, which can be accessed from the **Games** button on the bottom toolbar of the App Store.

Don't forget

For serious games players, the Arcade option in the App Store is worth looking at. This is accessed from the bottom toolbar in the App Store and is a monthly subscription service. It includes all of the latest Apple games, which you can play on your own or against other people, including those in your Family Sharing group.

11 Traveling Companion

This chapter shows how the iPad is an essential travel accessory, ideal when you are on the move. It looks at the Maps app for getting around, and a range of travel apps.

Beware

To ensure that the Maps app works most effectively, it has to be enabled in Location Services so that it can use your current location (**Settings** > **Privacy** > **Location Services** > **Maps** and select **While Using the App** under **Allow Location Access**).

Hot tip

Tap on the icon in Step 2 to change it into the active compass, below. With this activated, when you change position the map moves with you at the same time.

Looking Around Maps

With the Maps app you need never again wonder about where a location is, or worry about getting directions to somewhere. As long as you are connected to Wi-Fi or have a 5G/4G/3G network, you will be able to do the following:

- Search maps around the world.

- Find addresses, famous buildings or landmarks.

- Get directions between different locations.

- View traffic conditions.

Viewing maps
To view your current location:

1 Tap once on the **Maps** app

2 Tap once on this button to view your current location

3 Double-tap on a map with one finger to zoom in (or swipe outwards with thumb and forefinger)

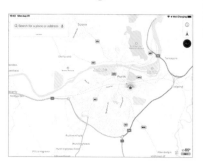

4 Tap once with two fingers on a map to zoom out (or pinch inwards with thumb and forefinger)

Finding Locations

Within Maps you can search for addresses, locations, landmarks or businesses. To do this:

1 The Search box is at the top of the window

2 Enter an item into the Search box. As you type, suggestions appear underneath. Tap on one to go to that location

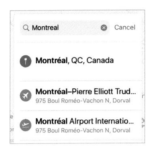

3 The location is shown on the map, and there is information about it in the left-hand panel

4 For your current location, categories for searching over items such as food outlets, shops and entertainment are available when you first tap in the Search box. Tap on one of these to see results for that category in the current location, and tap on specific items to view their own details

Tap on the **i** button in the top right-hand corner of any map, to access the Maps settings. This can be used to display the default **Map** style and also **Transit** and **Satellite**.

You can also search for locations by postcode or zip code.

Some locations provide a 3D Flyover tour. If this is available, a **Flyover** button will be displayed in Step 3.

Getting Directions

Finding your way around is an important element of using maps. This can be done with the Directions function:

Hot tip

Below the Maps Search box are options for adding favorite locations. Tap once on a location to add its details or tap once on the **Add** button to include a new location.

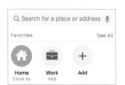

1 Tap once in the Search box at the top of the window

2 Enter the destination and tap on one of the results (by default, the directions will be given from your current location)

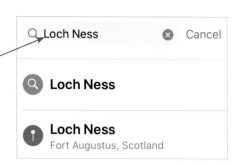

3 Tap once on the **Directions** button

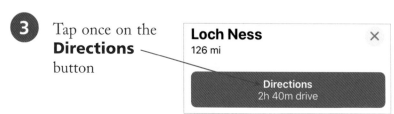

4 The route is shown on the map

Hot tip

For some destinations alternative routes will be displayed, depending on distance and traffic conditions. Tap on the alternative route to select it, and tap on the **Go** button to proceed.

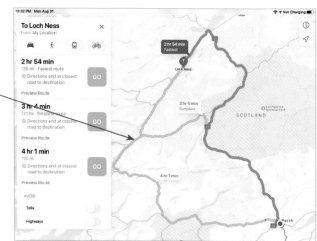

5 Tap on each of these buttons at the bottom of the window to view the route for **Drive**, **Walk**, **Transit** or **Cycle**

Directions for cycling is a new feature in iPadOS 14, but it is not currently available for all locations.

6 Tap once on the **Go** button to start the directions and view step-by-step instructions on the map

7 The route is displayed, starting from your current location. Audio instructions tell you the directions to be followed. As you follow the route, the map and instructions are updated

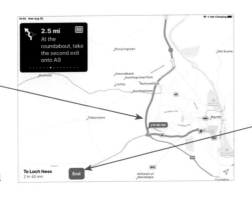

Don't forget

To get back to the Start view, tap once on the **End** button.

173

8 Swipe up from here to access options for the **Overview** or **Details** of the route. The Details option provides a step-by-step view of the route

A small number of cities have a selection of recommendations available within the Maps app. These are known as Guides and are available for San Francisco, London, New York and Los Angeles. When you search for one of these cities, the Guide will be available in the results. This is a new feature in iPadOS 14.

Traveling with your iPad

When you go traveling, there are a few essentials that you have to consider: passport, money and insurance, to name three. To this you can add your iPad: it is a perfect traveling companion that can help you plan your trip and keep you informed and entertained when you are away from home.

Uses for traveling

There are a lot of App Store apps that can be used for different aspects of traveling. However, the built-in apps can also be put to good use before and during your travels:

- **Notes**. Create lists of items to pack or landmarks that you want to visit.

- **Contacts**. Keep your Contacts app up-to-date so that you can use it to send postcards to friends and family. You can also use it to access phone numbers if you want to phone home.

- **Reminders**. Set reminders for important tasks such as changing foreign currency and buying tickets, and for details of flights.

- **Music**. Use this app to play your favorite music while you are traveling or relaxing at your destination.

- **Photos**. Store photos of your trip with this app and play them back as a slideshow when you get home.

- **FaceTime**. If you have a Wi-Fi connection at your destination you will be able to keep in touch using video calls (as long as the recipient has FaceTime too).

- **Books**. Instead of dragging lots of heavy books around, use this app as your vacation library.

174

Planning your Trip

A lot of the fun and excitement of going on vacation and traveling is in the planning. The anticipation of researching new places to visit and explore can whet the appetite for what is ahead. The good news is, you can plan your whole itinerary while sitting in an armchair with your iPad on your lap. In the App Store there are apps for organizing your itinerary, and others for exploring the possibilities of where you can go:

TripIt

This is an app for keeping all of your travel details in one place. You have to register, which is free, and you can then enter your own itinerary details. Whenever you receive an email confirmation for a flight, hotel or car hire that you have booked, you can email this to your TripIt account and this will be added to your itinerary.

GetPacked

A great way to get peace of mind before you leave. This app generates a packing list and to-do lists to check before you leave, based on questions that you answer about your vacation and travel arrangements. You can then select items to include on your packing list, from clothes to documents and medical items.

Cool Escapes Maldives

For a little bit of luxury, try this app that enables you to search for hotels, restaurants and bars; view breathtaking photos; and get insider tips for this idyllic destination.

World atlas & world map

A comprehensive travel companion that offers a world atlas containing information about countries, cities, landmarks, airports and events. Navigate around the atlas with the same swiping and tapping gestures as the Maps app. Tap on an item to access a wealth of information about it.

Although there is a small fee for the **GetPacked** app, it is well worth it, as it covers everything you will need to consider before you leave.

Some map apps are free to download but then there is a fee to buy some of the associated maps.

Viewing Flights

Flying is a common part of modern travel, and although you do not have to book separate flights for a vacation (if it is part of a package) there are a number of apps for booking flights and also following the progress of those in the air:

Skyscanner

This app can be used to find flights at airports around the world. Enter your details such as the departure airport, destination and dates of travel. The results show a range of available options, covering different price ranges.

Flightradar24

If you like viewing the paths of flights that are in the air, or need to check if flights are going to be delayed, this app provides this real-time information. Flights are shown according to flight number and airline.

Flight apps need to have an internet connection in order to show real-time flight information.

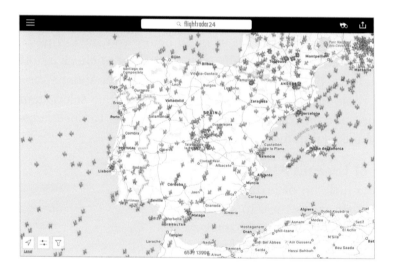

FlightAware Flight Tracker

Another app for tracking flights, showing arrivals and departures and also information about delays.

Finding Hotels

The internet is a perfect vehicle for finding good-value hotel rooms around the world. When hotels have spare capacity, this can quickly be relayed to associated websites, where users can usually benefit from cheap prices and special offers. There are plenty of apps that have details of thousands of hotels around the world, such as:

Tripadvisor
One of the top travel apps, this not only has hotel information but also restaurants, activities and flights. Enter a destination in the Search box and then navigate through the available options.

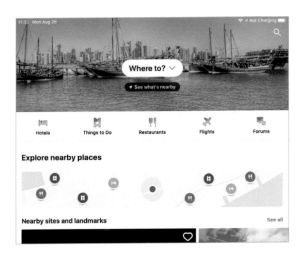

Hotels.com
A stylish app that enables you to enter search keywords for finding hotels based on destination, hotel name or nearby landmarks.

Booking.com Travel Deals
Another good, fully-featured hotel app that provides a comprehensive service and excellent prices.

lastminute.com
An app that specializes in getting the best prices by dealing with rooms that are available at short notice. Some genuine bargains can be found here, for hotels of all categories.

Hot tip

When booking flights and hotels, look up the price on your iPad, but check it on other, non-Apple, devices too; e.g. a Windows computer. Sometimes, different prices are displayed for searches from different types of devices.

Hot tip

Most hotel apps have reviews of all of the listed establishments. It is always worth reading these, as it gives you views from the people who have actually been there.

Converting Currency

Money is always important in life, and never more so than when you are on vacation and possibly following a budget. It is therefore imperative to know the exchange rate of currencies in different countries compared with your own. Two apps that provide this service are:

XE Currency & Money Transfer

This app delivers information about exchange rates for all major world currencies and also a wealth of background information, such as high and low rates and historical charts.

Beware

When changing currency, either at home or abroad, always shop around to get the best rate. Using credit cards abroad usually attracts a supplementary charge too.

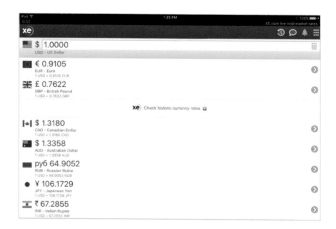

Currency

This app provides up-to-date exchange rates for over 150 currencies and 100 countries.

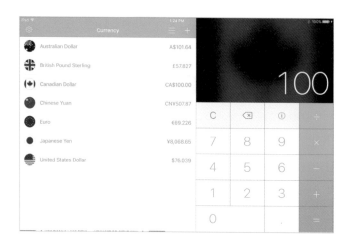

Travel Apps

Everyone has different priorities and preferences when they are on vacation. The following are some apps from the App Store that cover a range of activities and services:

- **Cities of the World Photo-Quiz**. An app to stimulate your wanderlust, with photo quizzes for recognizing over 110 famous cities. There are different types of quizzes, and also flashcards that provide the answers for you.

- **Disneyland Paris**. If you are entertaining your grandchildren at Disneyland Paris, this app will help you survive the experience. Maps, show times and descriptions of features help you organize all aspects of your visit.

- **Florida State Parks & Areas**. An extensive guide to the outdoor attractions of the Florida State Parks, including general information about all of the parks, advanced GPS maps and a built-in compass.

- **Google Earth**. Not just a travel aid, this app enables you to search the globe and look at photos and 3D maps of all your favorite places.

- **KAYAK**. A useful all-round app that compares hundreds of travel websites to get the best prices for flights, hotels and car rental. You can also create your own itineraries.

- **Language apps**. If you want to learn a new language for your travels, there is a wide range of apps to do this. These are located in either the Travel or Education categories in the App Store.

- **Magnifying Glass with Light**. Not just for traveling, this app acts as a torch and a magnifying glass all in one.

- **National Geographic Traveler**. Subscribe to this app to get an endless supply of high-quality travel features, photography and travel ideas.

- **New York Subway MTA Map**. Use this app to help you get around the Big Apple via the Subway. Plan your journeys and view live updates about stations and routes.

If you cannot find a certain app in the search results in the App Store, tap once on the **Filters** button, to the left of the Search box, and select the **Supports > iPhone Only** option. These apps can be downloaded for the iPad too, although they will have a smaller screen area to view the app.

There are several travel apps that have the functionality to mark locations around the world that you have visited. In the **Travel** section of the App Store, enter **places visited** (or similar) into the Search box, to view the matching apps.

...cont'd

The **Phrasebook** app comes with one free language. After that, you have to pay a small fee for each language that you want to use.

There are apps for displaying train times and details, but these are usually specific to your geographical location rather than covering a range of different countries.

- **Paris Travel Guide and Map**. A free map app for travel options around one of the great cities in the world.

- **Phrasebook**. Keep up with what the locals are saying in different countries with this app, which has useful phrases in 25 languages.

- **Places Around Me**. Find a variety of different places near to your current location, wherever you are in the world. The app can be used to locate restaurants, hotels, banks, ATMs and a host of other useful establishments, relative to your current location.

- **Royal Caribbean International**. Find some of your favorite cruises with this app, which displays the full brochure of P&O Cruises.

- **SIXT rent share and taxi**. Use this app for car rental, car sharing and taxis in over 100 countries.

- **Translate Free**. If you do not have the time or inclination to learn a new language, try this app to translate over 26 different languages.

- **Tube Map - London Underground**. Find your way around with this digital version of the iconic Tube Map. It includes live departure boards and station information.

- **Weather Live**. An app for showing the weather in locations around the world, with graphically-appealing forecasts, including extended forecasts for any coming day of the week or hour.

- **WiFi Connect**. It is always useful to be able to access Wi-Fi when you are on vacation, and sometimes essential. This app locates Wi-Fi hotspots in over two million locations worldwide.

- **Yelp: Local Food & Services**. Covering a range of information, this app locates restaurants, shops, services and places of interest in cities around the world.

12 Practical Matters

This chapter looks at practical issues, such as finding a lost device.

Finding your iPad

No-one likes to think the worst, but if your iPad is lost or stolen, help is at hand. The Find My iPad function (operated through the iCloud service) allows you to send a message and an alert to a lost iPad, and also remotely lock it or even wipe its contents. This gives added peace of mind, knowing that even if your iPad is lost or stolen, its contents will not necessarily be compromised. To set up Find My iPad (before it becomes lost or stolen):

Hot tip

Location Services must be turned **On** to enable the Find My iPad service (**Settings** > **Privacy** > **Location Services** and turn **Location Services On**).

1 Tap once on the **Settings** app

2 Tap once on the **Apple ID** account option

3 Tap once on the **iCloud** button

4 Tap once on the **Find My** option

5 Tap once on **Find My iPad** and drag the **Find My iPad** button **On** to be able to find your iPad on a map

Finding a lost iPad

Once you have set up Find My iPad you can search for it through the iCloud service, using another device. To do this:

Hot tip

Another app that can be used to find a lost device is **Lookout Mobile Security**, which can be downloaded from the App Store.

1 Log in to your iCloud account at **www.icloud.com**

2 Click once on the **Find iPhone** button (this also works for the iPad)

3 Click once on the **All Devices** button and select your iPad. It is identified, and its current location is displayed on the map

4 Click once on the green circle to view details about when your iPad was located

5 Click once here to send a sound alert to your iPad. This can be useful if you have lost it in the house or close by

6 Click once here to lock your iPad

7 Enter a message that will appear on the iPad. Its existing 6-digit passcode will then be required to unlock it (if it does not have one, you will be prompted to add one)

Click once on the **Erase iPad** button in Step 5 to delete the iPad's contents. It is extremely important to have previously backed up your iPad content using iCloud (**Settings** > **Apple ID** > **iCloud** > **iCloud Backup** > **On**) so that you can restore the content to a new device, or your original one if it is found.

If you are using Family Sharing (see pages 71-74) you can use the **Find My** app to locate the devices of other Family Sharing members.

Avoiding Viruses

As far as security from viruses on the iPad is concerned, there is good news and bad news:

- The good news is that, due to its architecture, most apps on the iPad do not communicate with each other so, even if there were a virus, it is unlikely that it would infect the whole iPad. Also, there are relatively few viruses being aimed at the iPad, particularly compared with those for Windows PCs.

- The bad news is that no computer system is immune from viruses and malware, and complacency is one of the biggest enemies of computer security. There have been some instances of photos in iCloud being accessed and hacked, but this was more to do with password security, or lack of, rather than viruses.

iPad security

Apple takes security on the iPad very seriously, and one way that this manifests itself is in the fact it is designed so that different apps do not talk to each other. This means that if there were a virus in an app, it would be hard for it to transfer to other apps and therefore spread across the iPad. Apple checks apps very rigorously, but even this is not foolproof, as shown in various attacks that have taken place against Apple devices.

Antivirus options

There are a few apps in the App Store that deal with antivirus issues, but do not actually remove viruses:

- **McAfee**. The online security firm has a number of apps that cover issues such as privacy of data and password security.

- **Norton**. Another popular online security option that has a range of apps to check for viruses and malware.

- **F-Secure SAFE**. Although not an antivirus app, this can be used to check websites that you are browsing, to alert you to suspicious sites and keep your details secure.

Don't forget

Malware is short for malicious software, designed to harm your computer, or access and distribute information from it.

Don't forget

Apple also checks apps that are provided through the App Store, and this process is very robust. This does not mean that it is impossible for a virus to infect the iPad, so keep an eye on the Apple website to see if there are any details about iPad viruses.

Dealing with Money

We all like to keep track of our money and, although it may not be as much fun as reading books or looking at photos, it is a necessary task that can be undertaken on the iPad.

Some general financial apps are looked at on page 186, but one of the most common platforms for financial matters is online banking. This is where you can use banking apps from your account provider to access your bank accounts. (Online banking sites can also be accessed through the web using Safari.)

Banking apps are tailored to your geographical location; i.e. the banks that operate in your country. Most banking apps operate in a similar way:

Beware

If you are logging in to your online banking service, make sure any "Remember Me" login details options are unchecked, particularly if other people have access to your iPad.

1. You have to first register for the online service. Once you have done this, tap on the **Log On** button to enter your account details

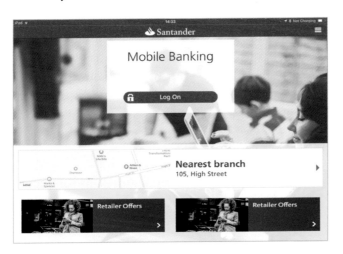

Don't forget

If you are looking to move home, there are a lot of real-estate apps that provide high-quality color photos of all parts of properties for sale. As with banking apps, real-estate apps are tailored to your geographical location and they all have a Search facility for looking for properties in different areas. The search results can usually be filtered by criteria such as price, number of bedrooms and property type.

2. You can now access your bank accounts, view balances and transfer money. General information is also available through the app, such as branch locations and contact details

Financial Apps

Within the Finance category of the App Store there are apps for managing your personal finances, viewing share prices, and organizing your bank accounts and bills. Some to look at are:

- **Account Tracker**. A useful app for keeping track of your expenditure. It can be used to monitor multiple bank accounts and also set alerts and reminders for paying bills.

- **Bloomberg: Business News**. This is an app for following stocks and shares. You can add any shares that you own, and view live prices while markets are open (with a 15-minute delay). There is also a financial news service.

- **Calculator**. For working out your own finances, there are several calculators providing large, attractive interfaces with plenty of functionality.

- **HomeBudget**. An app for managing your household income and expenses. It also supports charts and graphs so you can compare expenditure over periods of time.

- **Meter Readings**. Useful for keeping an eye on your home fuel consumption, this app helps you to save money by monitoring your utility readings. Enter the readings, and your usage and costs are displayed in user-friendly graphs to show where savings can be made.

- **Emma - Budget Planner Tracker**. As well as being used to manage bills and view all of your accounts, this app also provides useful planning features and reminders.

- **Pocket Expense**. Another in the range of apps with which you can monitor bank accounts, track bills, view transactions and see where you can save money.

- **Spending Tracker**. Another general finance app for managing your money and monitoring budgets.

- **My Stocks Portfolio Watchlist**. Another app for seeing how your share portfolio is doing. Real-time share information, market news and profit/loss details.

Hot tip

With your iPad and an internet connection, you should always be able to keep an eye on your shares portfolio, as well as buying and selling shares wherever you are.

Index